M3 MACBOOK

AIR

USER MANUAL

The Complete Guide With Comprehensive Illustrations For Beginners And Seniors On How To Setup & Use Your MacBook Air With Tips & Tricks For MacOS 14

BY

Williams M. Brown

Table Of Contents

INTRODUCTION

Following 2023's M3 chip's impressive performance and the addition of cutting-edge silicon to the MacBook Pro series, Apple has now introduced the M3 MacBook Air, a more budget-friendly and compact option.

The new M3 MacBook Air, which was unveiled on March 4 and will be released on March 8, comes in two sizes: 13 and 15 inches. Because this is mostly an update to the CPU, there aren't many improvements over previous versions; as a result, M2 users won't be enticed to upgrade just yet. Having said that, both remain committed to being powerful devices with terrific all-day battery life and a cherished physical factor that was first released in 2022. In a departure from the last generation, Apple has introduced the 15-inch and 13-inch versions at the same time. The 15-inch model was introduced last year, one year after the 13-inch variant.

M3 MacBook Air: Release Date

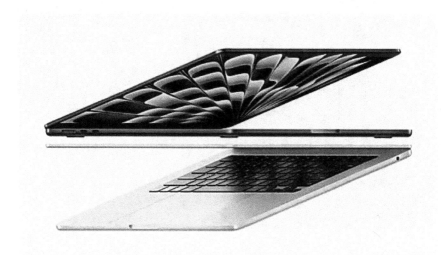

The delivery date of the M3 MacBook Air, which was announced in a press release on March 4 with little fanfare, is March 8.

M3 MacBook Air: Processor

Having previously been introduced by Apple in 2023, the new M3 CPU is the most significant update to the MacBook Air for 2024. The M3 is the first Apple silicon chip to use the new architecture, which is based on the 3-nanometer technology. This, in a nutshell, implies that the chips are denser, meaning that they can fit more transistors into a given area. This implies that they are much more efficient than the previous generation while maintaining the same speed, and they are also quicker at the same power consumption as M2.

Similar to the M2, the M3 chip's design consists of efficiency and performance cores. Apple claims that compared to the M2, the efficiency cores of the M3 are 30% quicker and the performance cores are 15% faster. Early benchmarks for the M3 MacBook Air show a general performance improvement of around 20%. Compared to its predecessor, the M3 CPU has a 60 percent faster Neural Engine, 2.5 times quicker rendering, and 5 billion more transistors.

In addition to improved graphics speed and more lifelike lighting, shadows, and reflections, the M3 processor introduces hardware-accelerated ray-tracing to Apple silicon.

This time around, Apple was eager to showcase the MacBook Air as the "world's best consumer laptop for AI." The aforementioned Neural Engine supports machine learning on macOS Sonoma. This linguistic shift is an attempt by Apple to signal that the company is shifting its focus to accommodate new developments in computing, most notably LLMs like ChatGPT and others. Apple did showcase several fantastic third-party applications that use AI and machine learning on macOS, such as Pixelmator Pro, Adobe Firefly, Microsoft 365, and Canva, but we don't anticipate any of their own AI initiatives to surface till WWDC 2024 and macOS 15.

M3 MacBook Air: Size And Weight

Like its predecessor, the M2 MacBook Air, the M3 is compact and lightweight. That works out to 2.7 and 3.3 pounds for the 13-inch and 15-inch versions, respectively. When measured in inches, the former is 0.44 in. tall, 11.97 in. broad, and 8.46 in. deep. At 0.45 inches thick, 13.40 inches wide, and 9.35 inches deep, the 15-inch model is only a little thicker.

M3 MacBook Air: Display

The display of the M3 MacBook Air is an IPS Liquid Retina LED screen. True Tone technology, broad color (P3), 500 nits of brightness, and 1 billion colors are all supported. The 13.6-inch model has a native resolution of 2560 by 1664 pixels at 224 pixels per inch, while the 15.3-inch model has a native resolution of 2880 by 1864 pixels at 224 pixels per inch.

M3 MacBook Air: Memory

You may get 16GB or 24GB of Unified Memory as upgrades for the M3 MacBook Air, with 8GB being the standard. As a general rule, every configuration step costs $200. For example, 16 GB of RAM is $200, and 25 GB is $400.

M3 MacBook Air: Storage

The M3 MacBook Air has 256 GB of solid-state drive (SSD) storage and 8 GB of Unified Memory as standard features. For $200, 1 terabyte, or 2 terabytes is available.

M3 MacBook Air: Audio And Camera

With the 13-inch M3 MacBook Air, you get the same four speakers and 1080p FaceTime HD camera as the previous generation. The M2 model's "wide stereo sound" is no longer supported by Apple, however the 13-and 15-inch devices' built-in speakers can play Spatial Audio with Dolby Atmos. Six speakers, including force-cancelling woofers, make up the audio system of the 15-inch model.

While the M3 MacBook Air still has a headphone port, it also has two microphone modes—Voice Isolation and Wide Spectrum—that enhance the sound quality of both audio and video conversations.

M3 MacBook Air: Connections And Ports

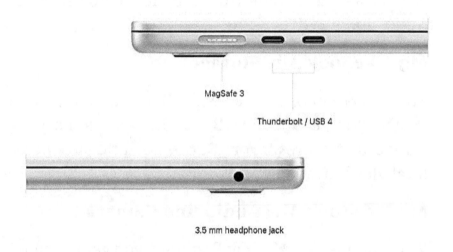

MagSafe 3

Thunderbolt / USB 4

3.5 mm headphone jack

The new M3 MacBook Air has the same features as its predecessor, including a headphone connector, a charging port for MagSafe 3, and two Thunderbolt/USB 4 connections that can handle data transfers of up to 40GB/s. Although the hardware connectors have remained same, the new M3 MacBook Air can accommodate two external displays (with the lid closed) instead of only one, as was the case with the M2 MacBook Air. The M3 MacBook Pro will also get this update from Apple. If you're looking for an external display that can handle 6K resolution at 60Hz, like the Pro Display XDR, the M3 MacBook Air is a great choice. With the cover closed, you can attach a second external display—like the Apple Studio Display—that can achieve a resolution of up to 5K at 60Hz.

In addition to Wi-Fi 6E, the M3 MacBook Air has Bluetooth 5.3, so you can hook up all your preferred accessories. Better, more consistent Wi-Fi speeds and, with a compatible router, less latency, as compared to the M2 model's Wi-Fi 6.

M3 MacBook Air: Price

Apple's M3 MacBook line follows the same price structure as the M2 line that came before it. So, the 13-inch model begins at $1,099 and the 15-inch model costs $1,299.

The 13-inch basic model comes with the 8-core CPU, 8-core GPU version of the M3 processor, 256GB of SSD storage, and 8GB of Unified Memory. Extra storage space (512GB) and a more powerful 10-core GPU are available for $1,299 extra. Pricing begins at $1,499 for the 16GB RAM option.

An 8GB Unified Memory, 256GB SSD, and the aforementioned 10-core GPU version of the M3 processor are the basic components of the $1,299 15-inch variant. Both the 512GB and 16GB memory versions start at $1,499, with the former starting at $1,699.

M3 MacBook Air: Colors

The color palette of the M3 MacBook Airs is identical to that of prior years, and upon launch, you'll have the following options:

- Space Grey
- Silver
- Midnight
- Starlight

WHAT'S NEW IN THE MACBOOK AIR M3
The M2 iteration of the MacBook Air, introduced by Apple last year, was a design overhaul. Its famous (although rather out-of-date) wedge shape was replaced with a flatter one, reminiscent to the MacBook Pro models. The new M3 MacBook Air design is carried over, with a weight of 2.7 pounds and a height of just 0.44 inches. On one side of that

narrow strip are two USB-C (Thunderbolt 3) connectors and a MagSafe 3 charging port, while on the other side is a 3.5mm headphone connection that supports headphones with high impedance. You may get it in Silver, Starlight, Space Grey, or Midnight (the colour pictured above) and it has dimensions of 11.97 inches broad by 8.46 inches long. There aren't any major surprises since, in the end, it feels just like a MacBook Air.

Introducing Wi-Fi 6E

The improvements aren't universally applicable, although they will help certain users. An improvement over the M2's Wi-Fi 6—now available in the M3—is the addition of Wi-Fi 6E. A Wi-Fi 6E router is required for the full performance enhancement.

Superior Assistance For External Monitors

With its lid closed, the MacBook Air can accommodate two high-resolution displays. There is a limit of one external display that the M2 model can accommodate. This may be exciting for those who, like myself, spend long periods of time seated at a desk. Having two large, complementary external monitors is clearly preferable than having one enormous screen and the MBA's little screen side by side on the desk, however the lid's need to be closed is a little strange.

Enhancements To Performance

The computer hardware is where the true meat and potatoes enhancements are found. Using the Apple M3 processor, this device claims to be considerably faster than its predecessors. Apple claims that the CPU and GPU will have slightly improved overall performance when compared to the M2. That is what rapid benchmarking tests imply. The purpose of these standards is just to serve as a reference; they will not be published online. Get the laptop with the highest score on the testing graphs by using one of the many excellent sites that provide controlled benchmark tests.

One of the most significant improvements to performance as a whole is the redesigned graphics processing unit architecture. This makes me feel a little torn since, of course, I'll always choose for the additional performance boost. A more powerful cooling system on the MacBook Pro will allow for even greater performance, so it's probably worth the additional money if you often play graphically intense games or undertake intensive creative tasks like video editing or music creation.

Widgets On Your Desktop

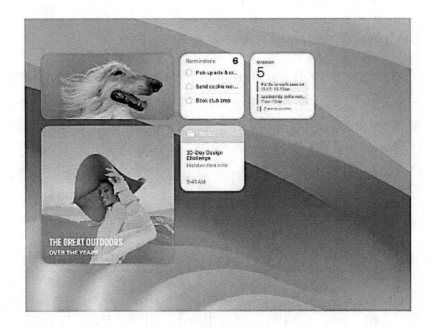

To make your favourite programmes even more accessible, you may add widgets to your desktop. Continuity also lets you use your iPhone's widgets on your Mac, saving you the trouble of installing separate programmes.

Video Conferencing

To combine your shared screen with your video, use Presenter Overlay. Use a hand gesture to add 3D effects to the chat, such as hearts, confetti, or fireworks. Right from the current window, you may share one app or many applications. When shooting with a Studio Display or an iPhone, you have complete creative control over the final product.

Personalize Your Reminders By Adding Columns And Sections.

Create sections for related reminders and decide whether to display them in columns. In addition, making shopping lists that categorize products is a breeze.

Use Safari's Web Applications And Profiles To Streamline Your Online Surfing Experience.

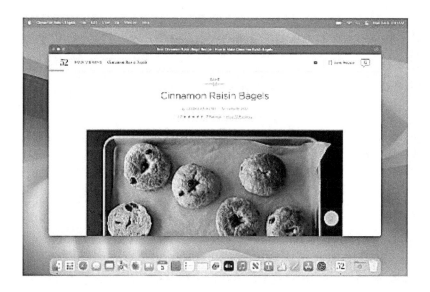

You can turn all of your favourite websites into applications and then access them from the Dock at any time. Enjoy the security of improved private browsing and create a profile to separate your personal and professional life.

And More Features

Find out more about macOS Sonoma: Among other things, you may set a slow-motion screen saver of a landscape, cityscape, or seascape as your wallpaper, connect notes, exchange passwords and passkeys with a trusted group of contacts, automatically prioritize your Mac's CPU and GPU for games in Game Mode, and much more.

WHAT'S INCLUDED WITH YOUR MACBOOK AIR

In addition to the cable and power adapter that come with your MacBook Air, you will also need one of the ones mentioned below in order to use it.

Accessory	Description
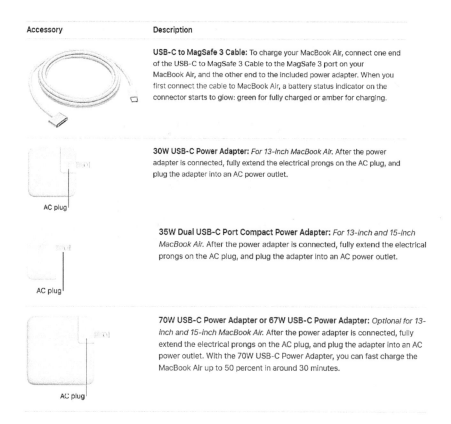	**USB-C to MagSafe 3 Cable:** To charge your MacBook Air, connect one end of the USB-C to MagSafe 3 Cable to the MagSafe 3 port on your MacBook Air, and the other end to the included power adapter. When you first connect the cable to MacBook Air, a battery status indicator on the connector starts to glow: green for fully charged or amber for charging.
AC plug	**30W USB-C Power Adapter:** *For 13-inch MacBook Air.* After the power adapter is connected, fully extend the electrical prongs on the AC plug, and plug the adapter into an AC power outlet.
AC plug	**35W Dual USB-C Port Compact Power Adapter:** *For 13-inch and 15-inch MacBook Air.* After the power adapter is connected, fully extend the electrical prongs on the AC plug, and plug the adapter into an AC power outlet.
AC plug	**70W USB-C Power Adapter or 67W USB-C Power Adapter:** *Optional for 13-inch and 15-inch MacBook Air.* After the power adapter is connected, fully extend the electrical prongs on the AC plug, and plug the adapter into an AC power outlet. With the 70W USB-C Power Adapter, you can fast charge the MacBook Air up to 50 percent in around 30 minutes.

You may purchase more accessories and adapters on an individual basis.

HOW TO USE MAGIC KEYBOARD FOR MACBOARD AIR

Emoji typing, language switching, locking your MacBook Air, and accessing a plethora of system operations are all made very simple with the Magic Keyboard with Touch ID's built-in capabilities. After configuring Touch ID, you'll be able to use your fingerprint to open your MacBook Air, lock the screen with a single tap, and pay for apps, books, and TV shows via Apple Pay and other online stores.

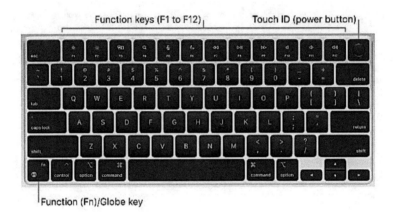

Function keys (F1 to F12)

Touch ID (power button)

Function (Fn)/Globe key

Get Touch ID Set Up. Touch ID may be configured either during setup or later on in the System Settings app under Touch ID & Password. Refer to the macOS User Guide's section on "Use Touch ID on Mac" for more details on Touch ID.

The MacBook Air Must Be Turned On. To open the device, you may use the power button, Touch ID, or any other key.

Utilize Touch ID. After you've enabled Touch ID, your password will be required every time you boot up or restart the machine. Once you've logged in once, you'll just need to touch your finger gently on the Touch ID sensor to validate any further password requests inside the same session. Secure online transactions with Apple Pay may also be accomplished using Touch ID.

Ensure The Security Of Your Macbook Air. Lock your screen with a single press of the Touch ID button.

Silently Power Down Your iPad Pro. Select Apple menu > Shut off to power off your MacBook Air. Select Apple menu > Sleep to sleep your MacBook Air.

Utilize The Function Keys. These frequently used system functions may be quickly accessed using the function keys located on the top row:

- Controlling the screen's brightness is as simple as pressing the "Decrease brightness" or "Increase brightness" keys (F1, F2).
- To access the Mission Control menu, which includes all of your open windows and spaces, on your MacBook Air, use the F3 key.
- To access Spotlight and do a search on your MacBook Air, use the Spotlight key (F4).
- Press the microphone key to enable dictation—you may dictate text in any app that allows you to write, including as Messages, Mail, Pages, and more—with the help of Siri using the F5 key. Press and hold the

Microphone key until Siri is activated. Then, voice your request right away.

- Pressing the F6 key will toggle the Do Not Disturb feature on and off. Notifications will not be visible or audible on MacBook Air while Do Not Disturb is enabled, but they may be seen in Notification Centre at a later time. For additional information, visit the Notification Centre.
- Media (F7, F8, F9): To rewind a video, music, or slide show, use the Rewind key. To play or stop, press the Play/stop key. To fast-forward, press the Fast-forward key.
- Pressing the Mute key will turn off the sound from either the internal speakers or the 3.5 mm headphone port.
- To adjust the level of the sound coming from the internal speakers, the 3.5 mm headphone jack, or a Bluetooth audio device, press the Decrease volume key or the Increase volume key, respectively, on the keyboard (F11, F12).

Note: Some function keys have special app-specific actions or alternate uses; for instance, pressing F11 will hide all windows and reveal the desktop. By pressing and holding the Function (Fn)/Globe key in conjunction with a function key, you may access the alternate function that is linked to that key.

Personalize Your Keyboard. Navigate to System Settings and locate the Keyboard section on the sidebar. From there, you can adjust keyboard settings as well as those for the Function (Fn)/Globe key. Adjust the brightness and lighting of the keyboard, choose the input source, activate dictation, modify shortcuts, and more. Pressing the Function (Fn) or Globe key may display the emoji picker or Character Viewer, or you can choose between these options.

Make Use Of Symbols And Emojis. If you've enabled the emoji picker in the Keyboard settings, you may access it by pressing the Function (Fn)/Globe key. You may enter symbols like pictographs and browse emoji by category or use the search bar once the emoji picker is active.

Get To Know The Shortcuts On Your Keyboard. If you're using a MacBook Air, you can speed up specific operations by pressing key combinations, or you may mimic the actions of a mouse or trackpad. To copy and paste the chosen text, for instance, use Command-C. Then, click the desired location and press Command-V.

HOW TO USE THE MACBOOK AIR TRACKPAD

Use your MacBook Air's trackpad to execute a plethora of tasks, like navigating websites, zooming in on documents, rotating photographs, and much more. Pressure sensing capabilities enhance the Force Touch trackpad's already impressive degree of interaction. You can operate with more accuracy thanks to the trackpad's feedback—a little vibration lets you know when things are aligned as you drag or rotate them.

Gesture	Action
	Click: Press anywhere on the trackpad. Or enable "Tap to click" in Trackpad Settings, and simply tap.
	Force click: Click and then press deeper. You can use force click to look up more information—click a word to see its definition, or an address to see a preview that you can open in Maps.
	Secondary click (that is, right-click): Click with two fingers to open shortcut menus. If "Tap to click" is enabled, tap with two fingers. On the keyboard, press the Control key and click the trackpad.
	Two-finger scroll: Slide two fingers up or down to scroll.
	Pinch to zoom: Pinch your thumb and finger open or closed to zoom in or out of photos and webpages.
	Swipe to navigate: Swipe left or right with two fingers to flip through webpages, documents, and more—like turning a page in a book.
	Open Launchpad: Quickly open apps in Launchpad. Pinch closed with four or five fingers, then click an app to open it.
	Swipe between apps: To switch from one full-screen app to another, swipe left or right with three or four fingers.

Personalize Your Hand Movements. Look for "Track pad" on the left side of System Preferences. Here are some things you can do:

- Read up on every motion
- You may customize the click pressure to your liking.
- Determine whether pressure-sensing capabilities will be used.
- Manage the pace of tracking
- Personalize the trackpad in other ways

Hint: Adjust the click pressure in Trackpad Settings to a harder level if you notice you're accidentally pressing down on the mouse button too hard. Alternately, you may choose to "Tap with three fingers" under the "Look up & data detectors" menu instead of the default "Force Click with one finger."

HOW TO CHARGE THE MACBOOK AIR BATTERY

Any time your MacBook Air is plugged into an electrical outlet, the battery within will recharge.

Get The Battery Charged. Using the provided connection and power adapter, connect your MacBook Air to a power source.

Menu Bar Should Display Battery Status. Make it easy to access your battery settings and see current battery status by adding an icon to your menu bar. To display the battery status in the menu bar, open System Settings, select Control Centre, and then, on the right side, locate Battery. The menu bar may also display the battery % if you so like.

You May Adjust The Battery's Parameters. In System Settings, you'll find choices to customize your battery.

- **Optimized Battery Charging:** By analysing your typical charging pattern, this function learns to save power and extend the life of your battery. When it anticipates that you will be left plugged in for a long time, it tries to charge the battery to 80% before you unhook it. You may enable Optimised Battery Charging under System Settings by going to the Battery section, clicking the information button next to Battery Health, and finally, turning it on.

- **Low Power Mode:** Choose this option to lower your energy consumption. This is a smart choice for trips or long periods of time when you won't have access to electricity. Select Low Power Mode from the choices that appear after clicking Battery in the sidebar of System Settings.

Note: By selecting Options in the Battery Settings menu, you may modify several advanced options such as the battery display brightness, the prevention of automated napping, and the timing of wake-up for network access, among others.

Finally, Plug In The Power Adapter. The MacBook Air's battery may be charged using either the MagSafe 3 connector and a USB-C to MagSafe 3 cable attached to the power adapter, or one of the Thunderbolt ports and a USB-C charging cable.

Note: The MacBook Air may be rapidly charged to 50% in about 30 minutes using the USB-C to MagSafe 3 Cable in conjunction with the optional 70W USB-C Power Adapter.

See How Much Juice Is In The Battery. To check the charge or battery life, just look for the battery status indicator on the menu bar's right side. Another option is to access the battery settings in the system preferences.

Charging   Charged

Record Of Battery Life. To see your battery's consumption for the previous 24 hours or the last 10 days, go to System Settings and click on Battery.

Reduce Electricity Consumption. Turning down the screen brightness, minimizing applications, and unplugging unused peripherals are all ways to get more use out of your battery on a single charge. You may adjust your power preferences in System Settings by clicking the Battery icon in the sidebar. A connected device's battery life can be negatively affected if your MacBook Air is in sleep mode.

HOW TO ADAPTERS FOR YOUR MACBOOK AIR

For your MacBook Air, Apple offers a variety of adapters that may connect to power, external devices, screens, and more.

Cable or Adapter	Description
	USB-C to USB Adapter: Connect your MacBook Air to standard USB accessories.
	USB-C to Lightning Cable: Connect your iPhone or other iOS or iPadOS device to your MacBook Air for syncing and charging.
	USB-C Digital AV Multiport Adapter: Connect your MacBook Air to an HDMI display, while also connecting a standard USB device and a USB-C charge cable to charge your MacBook Air.
	USB-C VGA Multiport Adapter: Connect your MacBook Air to a VGA projector or display, while also connecting a standard USB device and a USB-C charge cable to charge your MacBook Air.
	Thunderbolt 3 (USB-C) to Thunderbolt 2 Adapter: Connect your MacBook Air to Thunderbolt 2 devices.

HOW TO USE ACCESSORIES WITH YOUR MACBOOK AIR

Various peripherals, including a variety of mice, trackpads, keyboards, and even wearables like AirPods, may be synced with your MacBook Air. Your MacBook Air has two ports for attaching peripherals: one for wireless Bluetooth connectivity and one for connecting cables to the various Thunderbolt 4 / USB-C and Thunderbolt / USB 4 connections.

Before Starting. Follow these steps before you attach any peripheral to your MacBook Air:

- Refer to the instructions that were provided with your attachment.
- Verify that you are using the appropriate cable if you want to connect via one. To connect the connection to your MacBook Air's Thunderbolt / USB 4 connector, you may also need an adaptor.
- Always use the most recent macOS version on your MacBook Air.

Connect A Wireless Accessory

Then Activate Bluetooth. From the main menu, choose the Control Centre icon. When Bluetooth is enabled, the symbol changes to blue. To activate Bluetooth, click on the grey symbol.

Connect A Bluetooth Device. Pairing a Bluetooth item with a MacBook Air is required for first usage. To check whether your attachment is prepared to connect, read the instructions carefully. For example, some accessories need you to turn on Bluetooth by flipping a switch. The accessory and your Mac must be nearby and both must be switched on.

When your device is prepared to connect, go to your Mac's System Preferences and find the Bluetooth option in the sidebar. After finding the accessory in the list of Nearby Devices, click on it to connect.

Link A Bluetooth Device. An attachment will sync with your MacBook Air the moment you pair it. By navigating to the Control Centre from the menu bar, selecting Bluetooth, and then clicking the arrow, you can see all of the Bluetooth devices that are linked to your MacBook Air. Connected accessories are those that have a blue symbol in the list.

Go to your Mac's System Preferences and then choose Bluetooth if your item isn't pairing automatically. Check the My Devices list to see whether the accessory is there. If the item doesn't show up, pair it by following the instructions.

Unplug Or Lose Track Of A Bluetooth Device. Navigate to your Mac's System Preferences, then choose Bluetooth, to detach a Bluetooth item. Highlight the attachment in the My Devices list and then choose Disconnect. Select the information icon beside the Bluetooth item, and then choose Forget This Device, to prevent your MacBook Air from automatically connecting to it.

Plug In A Magic Keyboard, Magic Trackpad, Or Magic Mouse. Use the cord that came with your Magic Mouse, Magic Trackpad, or Magic Keyboard to connect it to your MacBook Air. To make the green light appear, turn on your attachment by sliding its switch to the on position. After that, your Mac and the attachment will pair.

Once the accessory and MacBook Air have been linked, you may remove the cord and use the device's wireless functionality. With Bluetooth enabled, your Magic Mouse, Trackpad, or Keyboard will sync with your Mac without your having to do anything.

Link Your Apple AirPods To Your Macbook Air. Before you connect your AirPods to your Apple device, be sure to read the instructions on how to pair them.

Attach A Device To A Device Via A Cord

You may use a cable to attach some accessories to your MacBook Air. If the accessory and cable are compatible, you may also be able to charge it or transmit data while connected.

Be sure to refer to the included paperwork before you proceed to connect your item. Additionally, you may need to connect in an extra power source for some peripherals.

If you own an item that fits both your MacBook Air's Thunderbolt / USB 4 connector and the port on your accessory, then you may connect both using a single cable. You may use an adapter to connect the cable to your Mac if it doesn't have the correct connection.

HOW TO USE AN EXTERNAL DISPLAY WITH YOUR MACBOOK AIR

If you own an Apple Studio Display, projector, or television, you can connect it to your MacBook Air. You may output videos using the MacBook Air's Thunderbolt / USB 4 connections.

Before Starting

Before connecting it to the MacBook Air, make sure your display is turned on.

Be Sure You Use The Appropriate Cable With Your Screen. Before connecting your display, double-check the instructions that came with it and use the cable that came with it.

Locate The MacBook Air's Ports. Get to know your MacBook Air's ports before you hook up a monitor. See "Take a tour: MacBook Air" to get to know your device's ports and their placement.

Verify The Rules And Regulations. You can find out more about the display types that your MacBook Air is compatible with by looking at the Technical Specifications. To find Display Support, open System Settings, go to Help, and then pick MacBook Air Specifications. You may have to scroll a little bit to find it.

Get A Screen For Your MacBook Air

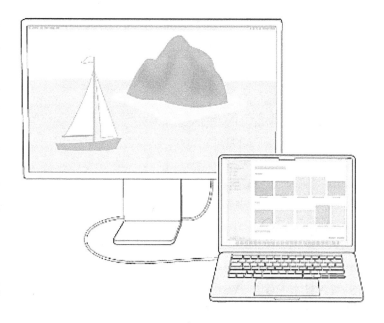

One external monitor up to 6K at 60 Hz or 4K at 144 Hz may be used with your MacBook Air. Find a Thunderbolt or USB 4 port and plug it into the screen.

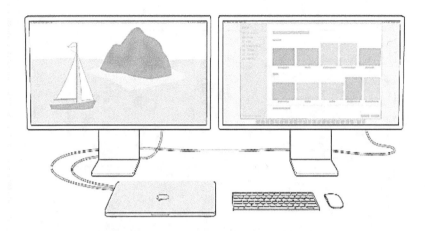

When the lid is closed, the MacBook Air with an M3 processor can accommodate up to two external screens, giving you even more workspace. Up to 6K at 60 Hz or 4K at 144 Hz can be supported by the main display, while the secondary display can support up to 5K at 60 Hz or 4K at 100 Hz. The second Thunderbolt / USB 4 port may be used to connect an additional external monitor. Connecting two external screens to a MacBook Air requires the lid to be closed, electricity, and an external keyboard, mouse, or trackpad.

- **Use Your MacBook Air With A Display Or Projector By Connecting It.** Your MacBook Air has many display and projector connector options. There is an adaptor available for purchase if the connection on the display cord does not fit the Thunderbolt /

USB 4 ports on your MacBook Air. This will allow you to connect the display.

- To use a USB-C display with a MacBook Air, plug it into one of the ports labeled Thunderbolt or USB 4.
- Your MacBook Air's Thunderbolt / USB 4 connector may be used to connect an HDMI monitor or TV with a USB-C Digital AV Multiport Adapter.
- If your MacBook Air has a Thunderbolt or USB 4 port, you may attach a VGA monitor or projector to it with a USB-C VGA Multiport Adapter.

For additional information or to make a purchase, you may visit apple.com, your neighborhood Apple Store, or other resellers. To ensure you choose the correct product, see the display's manual or get in touch with the manufacturer.

Apple TV May Be Used With Airplay. Using AirPlay, you may cast the display of your MacBook Air to an Apple TV-enabled television.

Once Your Display Is Connected,

Modify and organize the presentation. After you've attached a display or projector, go over to System Settings and choose Displays from the sidebar.

From there, you can rearrange the displays, select the one you want to use as your primary display and tweak the resolution and refresh rate (Hz). For optimal performance, use a lower resolution when increasing the refresh rate of your monitor.

If your MacBook Air has an M3 chip and you want to use two screens, the one you connect initially will be considered the main display. You may swap out the main screen by disconnecting and reconnecting them in a different sequence. Opening the lid on a MacBook Air with an M3 chip causes the laptop screen to take the place of the second display if you're using two displays.

To do screen mirroring, choose the display you want to use as a reflection, and then from the "Use as" menu, select the mirror option.

HOW TO SET UP YOUR MACBOOK AIR

During the setup process of your new MacBook Air, you will have the opportunity to personalize your Mac, enable features such as Touch ID, and initiate data transfers from other devices. You may be able to speed up the setup process for your new Mac by using your current settings if you already own an iPad, iPhone, or Mac.

If you want more assistance when configuring your Mac, you have the option to communicate with an Apple specialist by chat, email, phone, or by scheduling a visit to the Genius Bar.

With the help of Setup Assistant, configuring your Mac is a breeze. See When you've finished setting up your MacBook Air for the next instructions once setup is complete.

Click on the link below if you would like a detailed explanation of the procedure.

- For those unfamiliar with Mac
- Being an existing Mac user

HOW TO SET UP YOUR MACBOOK AIR FOR NEW USERS

This guide is meant to be used in conjunction with Setup Assistant and covers all of the setup steps.

Tip: Remember to scroll down to see all of the options for certain tasks. Just drag two fingers vertically on your trackpad to scroll if you're unfamiliar with using a Mac. Discover the ins and outs of the MacBook Air trackpad if you're interested in customizing gestures down the road.

Before Starting

- While setting up, it may be necessary to verify certain steps on another device, so have your iOS smartphone handy if you have one.
- During setup, you may use an other computer—for example, a Windows PC—to transfer data. Before you proceed, ensure that the computer you want to transfer data from has the most recent software version installed.
- The setup process for your MacBook Air is made simple using Setup Assistant and shouldn't take long at all. Be sure to allocate extra time if you want to transmit data.

Choose Your Language, Nation, Or Area, And Establish A Wi-Fi Connection.

Make Your Language Choice. Your Mac's language will be configured. Launch System Preferences, locate the Language & Region section in the sidebar, and make your selections to change the language at a later time.

Determine Your Location. Dates, currencies, temperatures, and more all be customized for your Mac in this way. If you want to make changes to your preferences at a later time, you may do so by opening System Preferences, clicking General in the sidebar, and then clicking Language & Region.

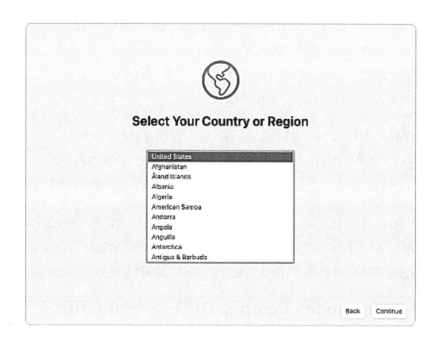

Please Enable The Accessibility Features. Click Not Now to skip to the Vision, Motor, Hearing, and Cognitive ability accessibility choices. Pressing the Escape key on your keyboard will bring up the VoiceOver setup menu on your Mac. Additional accessibility settings may be accessed by triple-clicking Touch ID, which is located on the upper right of your keyboard.

Find A Wi-Fi Hotspot. Select your Wi-Fi network and, if prompted, provide the password. You may also choose Other Network Options and adhere to the directions shown on the screen if you're using Ethernet. To link the Ethernet cable to the USB-C port on your MacBook Air, you'll need an extra Ethernet adapter, such as the Belkin USB-C to Gigabit Ethernet Adapter.

To modify the Wi-Fi network at a later time, launch System Settings, locate Wi-Fi in the sidebar, choose a network, and input the password if prompted.

Important: You may get an invitation to download macOS Mojave during setup. Proceed with the setup once you've followed the installation instructions.

Data Transfer From A Different Machine

From a Windows PC to a new Mac, you may transfer all of your data, including files, contacts, accounts, and more. Refer to Transfer data from another Mac if you're interested in transferring from another Mac. Wireless data transmission is also an option, or you may use an Ethernet connection to link your Windows PC to your MacBook Air.

Before Starting. Make sure you're running the most recent version of Windows on your computer. Afterward, get Migration Assistant for Windows.

Wireless Data Transfer. Make sure your new Mac and Windows PC are connected to the same

Wi-Fi network. To begin the setup process, locate your Windows PC and click on it.

Use An Ethernet Wire To Transmit Data. Use an Ethernet connection to link your Windows computer to your Mac straightaway. To attach the connection to your MacBook Air's USB-C port, you'll need an Ethernet converter like the Belkin USB-C to Gigabit Ethernet converter. Your Windows PC's port configuration will determine if an adapter is necessary to connect the Ethernet connection. Once you've connected them, go ahead and follow the setup screen's instructions by clicking on your Windows PC.

Move The Data At A Later Time. Another option is to forego data transmission right now. In such a case, go to the Migration Assistant window and choose Not Now. See Move your files to the new MacBook Air once you've set it up for instructions on how to do so.

Create An Account On Your Computer By Signing In With Your Apple ID.

Use Your Apple ID To Log In. An Apple ID is probably already in your possession if you own any other Apple product, such as an iPad or iPhone. You can sign up for an Apple ID right now (and it won't cost you a dime).

A combination of your email address and a password make up your Apple ID. Use it to access the App Store, the Apple TV app, iCloud, and all other Apple services. You should not confuse your Apple ID with the credentials you use to access your Mac account.

Advice: Use just your own Apple ID and don't give it out to anybody else.

Perform one of the following actions on this screen:

- **If You Have An Apple ID:** To access your Apple ID, type in your email address and password. An iOS device, such as an iPhone or iPad, is used to transmit verification codes. If you do not own an iOS device, a verification code may be sent to the mobile phone number linked to your Apple ID by text message. Just follow the on-screen instructions if you don't get the verification code or SMS.
- **If You Don't Have An Apple ID:** A new Apple ID may be created by clicking the "Create new Apple ID" button.

- **If You Have Forgotten Your Apple ID Or Password:** Click "Forgot Apple ID or password."
- **If You Don't Want To Sign In With Or Create An Apple ID At This Time:** Select "Set Up Later" if you'd rather not create or use an Apple ID right now. Sign in with your existing Apple ID or sign up for a new one after setup. Launch System Preferences and locate the "Sign in with your Apple ID" option on the sidebar.

Note: Readers should familiarise themselves with the terms and conditions after entering their Apple ID. Click Agree and then continue after checking the box to confirm.

Make An Account On A Computer. To set up an account that you may use to access your MacBook Air or authorize other operations, enter your name and then establish a password. To assist you in remembering your computer account password in case you ever forget it, you have the opportunity to add a hint. Tap it, and then choose a photo to use as your account's login.

Create a Computer Account

Fill out the following information to create your computer account.

Full name: Ashley Rice

Account name: ashleyrice

This will be the name of your home folder.

Password: new password   verify

Hint: optional

☑ Allow my Apple ID to reset this password

Back   Continue

Keep in mind that your Apple ID and your computer account are separate things. However, if you choose to use your Apple ID to change your Mac's password during setup, you may use your Apple ID if you forget the password.

Make This Your New MacBook Air

A screen known as "Make This Your New Mac" will display if you have previously set up another device running iOS 15 or later or iPadOS 15 or later using express setup. You won't see this step if your iPhone or iPad doesn't have the correct software version.

(Do you not know which iOS version your iOS device is running?)

By using the preferences saved in your iCloud account, Make This Your New Mac allows you to bypass a number of the setup procedures. Just click Continue to keep everything configured as it is. Touch ID and Apple Pay setup take precedence.

Click Customize Settings And On To The Next Step To Personalize Your New MacBook Air.

Enable Location Services: Turn on Screen Time, activate Siri, allow Location Services, and adjust your Mac's security and privacy settings. Select the option to enable location services, such as Maps, on your Mac. After opening System Settings, go to the Privacy & Security section on the sidebar, and finally, click on Location Services. From there, you may adjust your Location Services settings as needed.

You will be prompted to choose your time zone if you do not want to allow Location Services.

Inform Apple And Developers Of Your Analytics. Decide whether developers should be able to access crashes and use statistics shared by

Apple and whether to transmit diagnostics and data to Apple. After opening System Settings, go to Privacy & Security in the sidebar, then click Analytics & Improvements (you may have to scroll a little), and finally, choose the choices you want to use.

Prepare Screen Time. You can monitor your daily and weekly MacBook Air use with Screen Time, as well as control your children's screen time, establish app usage restrictions, and more. Click Continue to switch it on; alternatively, choose Set Up Later. Open System Settings and locate Screen Time in the sidebar. From there, you may pick your settings if you choose to set them up later.

Use FileVault To Protect Your Files. Protect your data using FileVault. To safeguard your data, you have the option to use FileVault during setup. Additionally, if you forget your disc password, you may authorize your iCloud account to unlock it.

Just Say "Hey Siri" To Activate Siri. During setup, you have the option to activate Siri and say "Hey Siri" to voice your requests to Siri. Select "Enable Ask Siri" to begin configuring Siri. When asked to set up "Hey Siri," just voice a series of instructions to Siri. Later, you may activate Siri and "Hey Siri" by going to System Settings, then clicking

Siri & Spotlight in the sidebar, and finally choosing your preferences.

To make Siri even better during setup, you may optionally choose to exchange audio with Apple. At a later time, you have the option to modify the sharing status of the audio. Navigate to System Settings, then choose Privacy & Security from the sidebar. Scroll down to Analytics & Improvements, and finally, select your preferences.

Integrate Apple Pay And Touch ID

Get Touch ID Set Up. To unlock your MacBook Air, authorize transactions with Apple Pay, and sign in to select third-party applications, you may add a fingerprint to Touch ID (the top-right button on your keyboard) during setup. To activate Touch ID, just follow the on-screen prompts. Launch System Preferences, then locate Touch ID & Password on the sidebar. Here you may configure Touch ID at a later time or add more fingerprints. Simply follow the on-screen prompts after clicking the Add button to add a fingerprint.

Set Up Apple Pay. You may link a debit, credit, or store card to your Apple Pay account and utilize Touch ID to make transactions once you set up Apple Pay. Follow the on-screen instructions to input your credit card information. You may be asked to validate your card if you have previously used it to buy media.

Select Wallet & Apple Pay from the System Settings menu to begin configuring Apple Pay or to add more cards at a later time. When prompted, follow the on-screen steps to activate Apple Pay.

Note: The ability to use your card with Apple Pay is subject to approval by the card issuer, who may need further information to complete the verification process. You can use Apple Pay with a lot of different debit and credit cards.

Customize The Look Of Your Desktop

Get The Style You Want. Choose from Light, Dark, or Auto to customize the look of your desktop. Open System Settings, choose Appearance, and then choose an option to modify the setting decision later on. Colors for highlights and sizes for icons in the sidebar are among the other look variables that you may choose.

Note: Make This Your New Mac's express setup option allows you to bypass this stage, so keep that in mind.

Setup Is Complete

A new MacBook Air is at your fingertips.

HOW TO SET UP YOUR MACBOOK AIR FOR CURRENT MAC USERS

This guide is meant to be used in conjunction with Setup Assistant and covers all of the setup steps.

Before Starting

- During setup, you may need to verify certain steps on another device, so have your second Mac, iPhone, or iPad nearby.
- During setup, you'll have the option to transfer data from another Mac. Before you proceed, ensure that the computer you want to transfer data from has the most recent software version installed.
- The setup process for your MacBook Air is made simple using Setup Assistant and shouldn't take long at all. Be sure to allocate extra time if you want to transmit data.

Choose Your Language, Nation, Or Area, And Establish A Wi-Fi Connection.

Make Your Language Choice. Your Mac's language will be configured. Launch System Preferences, locate the Language & Region section in the sidebar, and make your selections to change the language at a later time.

Determine Your Location. Dates, currencies, temperatures, and more all be customized for your Mac in this way. If you want to make changes to your preferences at a later time, you may do so by opening System Preferences, clicking General in the sidebar, and then clicking Language & Region.

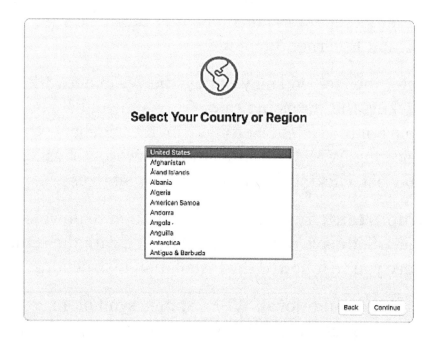

Please Enable The Accessibility Features. Click Not Now to skip to the Vision, Motor, Hearing, and Cognitive ability accessibility choices. Pressing the Esc key on your keyboard will bring up the VoiceOver setup menu on your Mac. To access even more accessibility settings, triple-click Touch ID.

Find A Wi-Fi Hotspot. Select your Wi-Fi network and, if prompted, provide the password. You may also choose Other Network Options and adhere to the directions shown on the screen if you're using Ethernet. To link the Ethernet cable to the USB-C port on your MacBook Air, you'll need an extra Ethernet adapter, such as the Belkin USB-C to Gigabit Ethernet Adapter.

After the fact, you may change the Wi-Fi network by clicking the status indicator (in the menu bar) or by going into System Settings (in the sidebar), then selecting Wi-Fi, entering the password (if asked), and last, clicking the network you want to use.

Important: You may get an invitation to download macOS Mojave during setup. Proceed with the setup once you've followed the installation instructions.

Tip: An additional Wi-Fi status symbol may be added to the menu bar after setup if it isn't already there. Find Control Centre in the sidebar of System Settings, click on it, and then choose "Show in Menu Bar" for Wi-Fi.

Data Transfer From A Different Mac

Transferring information from an old Mac to a new MacBook Air is possible. This includes files, contacts, accounts, and more. You may also use your Mac's startup disc or a Time Machine backup to move data. One option for transferring data from another Mac is to use wireless technology; another is to use an Ethernet connection to link your Mac to your MacBook Air.

Before Starting. Make sure the other Mac has the most recent software version. Once you're ready to begin the transfer, launch Migration Assistant on your previous Mac. In the Applications folder, you should find the Utilities folder, which is where you can find Migration Assistant.

Wireless Data Transfer. If your old Mac and new Mac are near one other, you can wirelessly transfer files between the two. Once the setup page appears, choose your second Mac and proceed with the on-screen prompts.

Use An Ethernet Wire To Transmit Data. Just plug in an Ethernet wire and link up your two Macs. An Ethernet adapter, such as the Belkin USB-C to Gigabit Ethernet Adapter, is required to link the Ethernet cable to the USB-C port on your MacBook Air. Depending on the ports on your second Mac, you may have to use an adaptor to link the Ethernet connection. Once they're linked, go to the setup page, find your second Mac, and click on it.

Move The Data At A Later Time. Another option is to forego data transmission right now. In such a case, go to the Migration Assistant window and choose Not Now. See Move your files to the new MacBook Air once you've set it up for instructions on how to do so.

Create An Account On Your Computer By Signing In With Your Apple ID.

Use Your Apple ID To Log In. You may use the verification code that you get on your other Apple devices when you sign in with your Apple ID during setup. On your brand-new MacBook Air, you should see a verification code; input it to continue. You have the option to have the verification code texted or called to you if you do not own the device or do not get it. Select "Can't use this number" and then follow the on-screen prompts if you are unable to use the phone number linked to your Apple ID.

To create a new Apple ID, tap "Create new Apple ID." Select "Forgot Apple ID or password" if you've misplaced either your Apple ID or password.

Press Set Up Later if you'd rather not log in or establish an Apple ID at this time. Sign in with your existing Apple ID or sign up for a new one after setup. Launch System Preferences and locate the "Sign in with your Apple ID" option on the sidebar.

Note: Readers should familiarize themselves with the terms and conditions after entering their Apple ID. Click Agree and then continue after checking the box to confirm.

Make An Account On A Computer. Create an account using your name and a password; this will allow you to access your MacBook Air and authorize future activities. To assist you in remembering your computer account password in case you ever forget it, you have the opportunity to add a hint. Tap it, and then choose a photo to use as your account's login.

Create a Computer Account

Fill out the following information to create your computer account.

Full name: Ashley Rice

Account name: ashleyrice

This will be the name of your home folder.

Password: new password | verify

Hint: optional

☑ Allow my Apple ID to reset this password

Back | Continue

Keep in mind that your Apple ID and your computer account are separate things. However, if you choose to use your Apple ID to change your Mac's password during setup, you may use your Apple ID if you forget the password.

Make This Your New Mac

An option to "Make This Your New Mac" will show up if you have already set up another device running iOS 15 or later, macOS 12 or later, or iPadOS 15 or later. This step is not visible if your Mac, iPad, or iPhone does not have the correct software version. (Do you not know which software version is installed on your iOS device?)

By using the preferences saved in your iCloud account, Make This Your New Mac allows you to bypass a number of the setup procedures. Just click Continue to keep everything configured as it is. Touch ID and Apple Pay setup take precedence.

Click Customise Settings And On To The Next Step To Personalise Your New MacBook Air.

Enable Location Services: Turn on Screen Time, activate Siri, allow Location Services, and adjust your Mac's security and privacy settings. Select the option to enable location services, such as Maps, on your Mac. After opening System Settings, go to the Privacy & Security section on the sidebar, and finally, click on Location Services. From there, you may adjust your Location Services settings as needed.

Selecting your time zone is the default behavior if you do not want to use location services.

Inform Apple And Developers Of Your Analytics. Decide whether developers should be able to access crashes and use statistics shared by Apple and whether to transmit diagnostics and data to Apple. After opening System Settings, go to Privacy & Security in the sidebar, then click Analytics & Improvements (you may have to scroll a little), and finally, choose the choices you want to use.

Prepare Screen Time. You can monitor your daily and weekly MacBook Air use with Screen Time, as well as control your children's screen time, establish app usage restrictions, and more. If you want to enable Screen Time now, click Continue; if not, choose Set Up Later. Open System Settings and locate Screen Time in the sidebar. From there, you may pick your settings if you choose to set them up later.

Use FileVault To Protect Your Files. Protect your data using FileVault. To safeguard your data, you have the option to use FileVault during setup. Additionally, if you forget your disc password, you may authorize your iCloud account to unlock it.

Just Say "Hey Siri" To Activate Siri. During setup, you have the option to activate Siri and say "Hey Siri" to voice your requests to Siri. Select "Enable Ask Siri" to begin configuring Siri. When asked to set up "Hey Siri," just voice a series of instructions to Siri. Later, you may activate Siri and "Hey Siri" by going to System Settings, then clicking Siri & Spotlight in the sidebar, and finally choosing your preferences. View Siri on a Mac for further information.

If you want Siri to be even better, you may choose to share audio with Apple. At a later time, you have the option to modify the sharing status of the audio. Navigate to System Settings, then choose Privacy & Security from the sidebar. Scroll down to Analytics & Improvements, and finally, select your preferences.

Integrate Apple Pay And Touch ID

Get Touch ID Set Up. Touch ID allows you to unlock your MacBook Air, allow transactions with Apple Pay, and sign into select third-party applications. You can even add a fingerprint to it. To activate Touch ID, just follow the on-screen prompts. Launch System Preferences, then locate Touch ID & Password on the sidebar. Here you may configure Touch ID at a later time or add more fingerprints. Simply follow the on-screen prompts after clicking the Add button to add a fingerprint.

Set Up Apple Pay. You may link a debit, credit, or store card to your Apple Pay account and utilize Touch ID to make transactions once you set up Apple Pay. Simply input your card information and follow the on-screen instructions. You may be asked to validate your card if you have previously used it to buy media.

Select Wallet & Apple Pay from the System Settings menu to begin configuring Apple Pay or to add more cards at a later time. When prompted, follow the on-screen steps to activate Apple Pay.

Note: The ability to use your card with Apple Pay is subject to approval by the card issuer, who may need further information to complete the verification process. You can use Apple Pay with a lot of different debit and credit cards.

Customize The Look Of Your Desktop

Get The Style You Want. Choose from Light, Dark, or Auto to customize the look of your desktop. Open System Settings, choose Appearance, and then choose an option to modify the setting decision later on. Colors for highlights and sizes for icons in the sidebar are among the other look variables that you may choose.

Note: Make This Your New Mac's express setup option allows you to bypass this stage, so keep that in mind.

Set Up Is Complete

A new MacBook Air is at your fingertips.

HOW TO USE APPLE ID ON MAC

All of Apple's services may be accessed using your Apple ID. Use your Apple ID for a plethora of services: the App Store, Apple Music, Apple Podcasts, Apple TV, and Apple Books; iCloud for content sync across devices; Family Sharing group creation; and much more.

Note: You won't have to start all over with an Apple ID just in case you lose access to your old one. To recover your password, just click the "Forgot Apple ID or password?" option located in the sign-in box.

Get an Apple ID for everyone in your family if they use Apple products. Later on, we'll go over how to set up Family Sharing so that you and your children may share purchases and subscriptions using their own Apple IDs.

Completely Centralised. Control all of your Apple ID's associated features from one location. Your MacBook Air's Apple ID and Family Sharing preferences may be found in the System Settings, which can be accessed from the sidebar. If you haven't done so previously, click "Sign in with your Apple ID" located at the top of the sidebar to sign in using Apple ID.

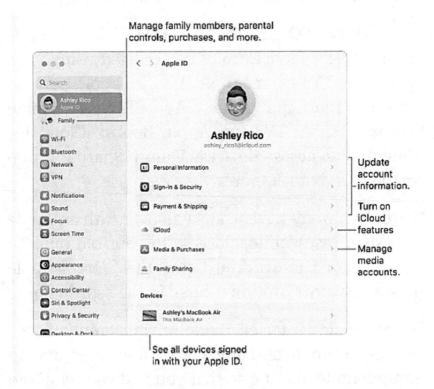

Manage family members, parental controls, purchases, and more.

Update account information.

Turn on iCloud features

Manage media accounts.

See all devices signed in with your Apple ID.

Revise Your Payment, Account, And Security Details. To access and edit your account details, go to System Preferences, click your Apple ID on the sidebar, and then choose an item.

- **Overview:** Get the lowdown on whether your account is all set up and running well. If it isn't, you'll notice some helpful hints and alerts here.
- **Personal information:** Modify your Apple ID-linked Memoji or picture, name, and birthday. Along with seeing your data management settings, you may customize your choices for Apple communications.
- Security & Sign-In: Modify the password for your Apple ID, enable two-factor authentication, modify the email and phone addresses that may be used to log in, and establish Account Recovery or Legacy Contact.
- **Payment And Shipping:** Managing your Apple ID's associated payment methods and delivery address is essential for making purchases in the Apple Store.
- **iCloud:** To enable or disable iCloud functionality, go to the iCloud menu and choose the option. Manage your iCloud storage and enable iCloud+ features. By enabling iCloud on one device and signing in with the same Apple ID on another, you have

access to all of your saved information in iCloud.

- **Media And Purchases:** Here you can adjust your subscriptions, choose your purchase options, and access your Apple Music, Podcasts, TV, and Books accounts.

View All Of Your Gadgets. View the full list of devices associated with your Apple ID. To check whether Find My [device] is enabled on all of your devices, go to Find My. whether you're using iOS or iPadOS, you can also check the status of iCloud

Backup. If you no longer possess a device, you may also delete it from your account.

Sharing Within The Family. Up to six people may be added to a family group via Family Sharing. After that, you may use Find My to report devices as missing or share their whereabouts. By creating Apple ID accounts and establishing Screen Time limitations, you can keep tabs on your children's device use.

Many Apple services, such as Apple TV+, Apple Music, iCloud, and more, allow subscribers to pool their resources via Family Sharing. Sharing purchases made in the iTunes Store, Apple Books, Apple TV app, and App Store is also possible. Everyone in the family may continue to utilize their iCloud accounts. Use your MacBook Air to authorize your children's purchases and pay for household items with a single credit card. Navigate to System Settings > Family to see and modify your Family Sharing preferences.

HOW TO USE ICLOUD WITH YOUR MACBOOK AIR

You can sync your data across all of your devices and easily share files using iCloud. When you utilize iCloud and sign in with the same Apple ID on your

MacBook Air, iPad, iPod touch, iPhone, and Apple Watch, everything works together without a hitch.

Navigate to System Preferences, then choose "Sign in with your Apple ID" from the sidebar. This will enable iCloud, which you may have neglected to enable during Mac setup. Select iCloud after logging in, and then toggle the iCloud functions to on or off.

Enjoy Your Content On Any Device. Keep all of your files up-to-date with iCloud's secure document, picture, and video storage, editing, and sharing capabilities across all of your devices.

Various Gadgets May Be Used With Your Macbook Air. With Continuity, you can easily transfer media from your MacBook Air to other devices. When your MacBook Air and other devices are near each other, you may easily sync and sync them using your Apple ID. A few examples are multitasking, AirPlay for screen streaming to other Macs or Apple TVs, Sidecar for working side by side with your MacBook Air, and many more. You can even use your iPhone as a camera for your MacBook Air.

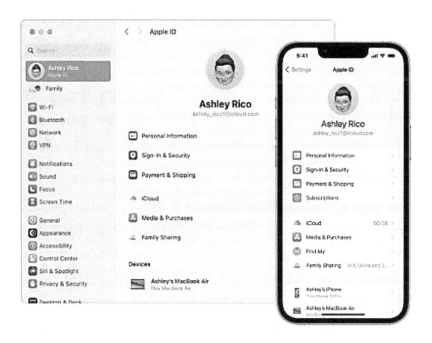

Leverage iCloud+ To Do More. Additional storage space for your photographs, files, and more is available with the subscription service iCloud+. The iCloud+ storage plan may be shared using the Family Sharing feature. With iCloud+, you get a lot more features, including HomeKit Secure Video, iCloud Private Relay, and the ability to use a custom domain with your iCloud.com email address.

HOW TO USE YOUR MAC TO ACCESS THE STUFF STORED IN ICLOUD.

With iCloud, you can ensure that all of your essential data, including images, documents, notes, and the iCloud Keychain, is always accessible, backed up, and secure across all of your devices. It comes standard on all Apple products and comes with 5 GB of storage space for everyone. (Your available space is not determined by purchases made from the App Store, Apple TV app, Apple Books, or iTunes Store.)

With an Apple ID and iCloud enabled, all you need is an iOS device—an iPhone, iPad, or iPod touch—to access all your content. If you're looking for more storage space and access to premium services like iCloud Private Relay, Hide My Email, Custom Email Domain, and HomeKit Secure Video compatibility, iCloud+ is a great option to consider.

Save All Of iCloud Drive Automatically. You may save files to your desktop or the Documents folder, and then they will be immediately saved on iCloud Drive, so you can view them from anywhere. The Files app for iOS devices, iCloud.com on the web, the iCloud for Windows software on Windows PCs, and the MacBook Air all provide access to the same iCloud Drive files. Your modifications to a file saved on your device or in iCloud Drive will be visible in any view of that file.

You may activate iCloud Drive by going to System Preferences, selecting your Apple ID from the sidebar, clicking iCloud, and finally, turning it on. For further information, go to the iCloud User Guide's section on Setting up and using iCloud Drive on all your devices.

You May Save And Share Pictures. You may access your picture library and all of your edited films and photographs from any device with iCloud storage. Activate iCloud Photos by opening System Preferences, navigating to your Apple ID in the sidebar, selecting iCloud, and finally, turning on Photos.

Upload media to iCloud Shared Photo Library and share them with up to five recipients. In a shared library, everyone may make modifications, such as adding new material, editing existing content, or commenting on existing information. Smart recommendations simplify the process of adding certain images from your library, such as those of a given period or starring a specific individual. Start by navigating to Photos > Settings. Then, choose the Shared Library option and proceed as instructed.

No Matter Where You Are, You Can Enjoy Your Purchases. All of your purchases from the App Store, Apple TV app, Apple Books, and iTunes Store will be accessible whenever you sign in with the same Apple ID, regardless of the device you used to make the purchase. That means you can take your whole media library with you wherever you go.

Your MacBook Air May Be Located Via Find My Mac. If you've enabled Find My Mac on your MacBook Air and it goes lost, you may use it to remotely wipe all of its data, lock its screen, and even find it on a map. Launch System Preferences, locate your Apple ID on the sidebar, choose iCloud, and then click Show All. From there, you can activate Find My Mac. When your Mac goes missing or is stolen, go to this page from Apple Support.

Note: If your MacBook Air is multi-user, only one of those accounts may activate Find My Mac.

HOW TO LEARN THE SYSTEM SETTINGS ON YOUR MACBOOK AIR

Personalize your MacBook Air to fit your requirements by adjusting the options under System options. You may manage and exchange passwords, modify the brightness or resolution using Display Settings, tweak Accessibility settings, and much more. For example, you can install a screen saver that doubles as a wallpaper. An updated version of the program is also available for download.

First, open System Settings by clicking the corresponding icon in the Dock or going to the Apple menu and selecting System Settings. Then, locate the option you want to modify and click on it in the sidebar. Scroll down to see all options in the sidebar.

Advice: Use the search bar to locate the specific parameter you need to change if you can't remember its name. In the sidebar, you may see the results as you write.

Choose the color
scheme for your Mac.

Click an item in the sidebar
to adjust settings.

Lock Your Screen. After a certain amount of inactivity, your MacBook Air has the option to either activate a screen saver or turn off the screen. When you go back to your Mac, you may lock the screen with a password if you choose. Get it set up by navigating to System Settings > Lock Screen.

Get A Screen Saver. When you're not using your MacBook Air, you may make the screen a beautiful piece of art using a slow-motion screen saver. The Screen Saver option is located in the System Preferences menu. You may also set a screen saver as your wallpaper by selecting "Show as wallpaper" while you're using a Landscape, Cityscape, Underwater, Earth, or Shuffle Aerials.

Keep Your Passwords Safe. You have the option to see your passwords in System Settings, whether you've saved them on your Mac or in iCloud Keychain. Enter your MacBook Air login credentials after clicking Passwords in the sidebar. After you click the information button, you can see your password for that specific site. Just hover your cursor over the password to show it. In addition to being able to change or remove passwords, you can also share them using AirDrop by clicking the information button.

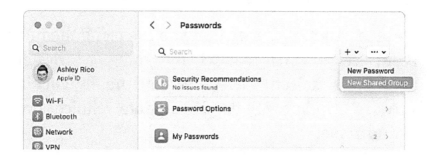

Never Give Out Your Passkey Or Password To Anybody. Assign a set of trusted contacts the ability to access the passkeys and passwords you want to share. Whenever you modify, your passkeys and passwords will automatically be updated. Press on Passwords once you've navigated to System Settings. After naming your group and clicking the Add button, you can begin adding members by selecting New Shared Group. Press Add once you've entered the names of the recipients you want to share with. You may create a group, then pick Move Passwords to a Group from the menu that appears. After that, choose the accounts you want to exchange passwords for, and finally, click Move.

Edit The Control Centre And Menu Bar To Your Liking. You may customize the appearance of the Control Centre and the menu bar by selecting the settings you like. Select Control Centre from the sidebar under System Settings. From there, you may **Adjust The Settings As You Want.**

Update MacOS. Verify that you are using the most recent version of macOS by going to System Preferences, selecting General, and finally clicking Software Update. Software update choices are customizable.

Family Sharing And iCloud Preferences. Access iCloud on your MacBook Air by signing in with your Apple ID. Control the way your applications use iCloud. Establish and oversee Family Sharing.

HOW TO DISPLAY SETTINGS FOR YOUR MACBOOK AIR

Adapt To The Ambient Light. True Tone is built into your MacBook Air. For a more realistic viewing experience, True Tone automatically adjusts the screen's color to match the ambient light. Go into System Preferences, Displays, and toggle True Tone on or off.

Implement A Dynamic Desktop. The time of day in your location is immediately reflected in the dynamic desktop image when you use it. Select a photo to use as Dynamic Desktop by clicking Wallpaper under System Settings. Turning on Location Services will cause your screen to adapt to your current time zone. Even without Location Services enabled, the image will adapt to the time zone you choose in the Date & Time preferences.

Modify The Way Things Show Up On Screen. To make things easier to view, you may change the display resolution to make the screen larger overall or to increase the size of text and icons. A simple shake of the mouse may also make the cursor more visible or help you find it faster.

Keep Your Mind Sharp In Dark Mode. All of the in-built macOS programs, as well as the desktop, menu bar, and Dock, are customizable to utilize a dark color scheme. By making the controls and windows darker, you can make your content stand out. To make it easier on the eyes while working in dark situations, applications like Mail, Contacts, Calendar, and Messages have white text on a black backdrop.

For experts in the field of picture editing, we have developed black Mode. With the black background of the program, colors, and tiny details stand out. Those who want to keep their attention only on their material will also find it useful.

Night Shift. When you're in low light or at night, you may lessen your exposure to blue light by changing your Mac's color scheme to something warmer. Warmer screen colors may aid in falling asleep, while blue light might make it more difficult to do so. You have the option to program Night Shift to activate and deactivate automatically at certain periods, or to activate from sunset to morning. To adjust the Night Shift, go to System Settings, select Displays, and then locate the button at the bottom of the page. To change the hue, simply drag the slider.

Run A Display Cable. A TV, projector, or external display may be attached to your Mac.

HOW TO TURN ON ACCESSIBILITY ON YOUR MAC

With the accessibility tools built into your Mac, any user may access and utilize all of Apple's features with ease. Launch System Settings and locate the Accessibility section on the sidebar. From there, you can use these features. There are five main types of accessibility settings:

- **Vision:** enlarge the pointer, apply color filters, and zoom in on the screen, among other things.

- **Auditory:** a variety of captioning options, including screen-based customization, Real-Time Text (RTT) call-making and receiving, live audio captioning, and more.
- **Accessibility:** Manage your Mac and its applications using voice commands, physical keys, an onscreen keyboard, gestures, or assistive devices.
- **Speech:** Just type in your words and they will be pronounced aloud. A unique voice may also be created by you.
- **General:** you may program shortcuts to activate and deactivate accessibility features with ease.

Feature Accessibility For Visual

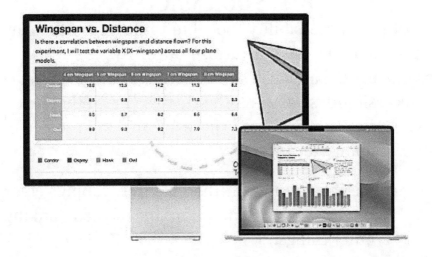

Zoom In Or Out To Suit Your Needs. Part or all of the screen may be zoomed in. With several displays, you may maintain different levels of magnification: one at a close range and another at a wider one. Select System Preferences from the Apple menu. In the System Preferences sidebar, locate Accessibility. On the right side, click Zoom to alter the zoom settings.

Take Use Of Voiceover, the in-built screen reader. With VoiceOver, you may hear the text in windows, documents, and websites read aloud. You may use the trackpad or keyboard to interact with your Mac while you use VoiceOver. A refreshable braille display is another option for usage with VoiceOver.

Additionally, VoiceOver allows you to:

- Make sure that VoiceOver can understand alternate picture descriptions.
- Enhance your PDF signatures with personalized descriptions.
- Use iCloud to save your punctuation marks.
- Select several braille tables from the International.

For VoiceOver, Use Siri. One may utilize Siri for VoiceOver or Speech if they like Siri's natural voice.

Choose one of these options to activate VoiceOver:

- Tap the Command key five times. Pressing the keys disables VoiceOver if it is currently active.
- Make use of Siri. Something along the lines of "Turn VoiceOver on" or "Turn VoiceOver off" would do.
- To use Touch ID on a Mac or Magic Keyboard, press and hold the Command key while pressing Touch ID three times in rapid succession.
- To access Accessibility, go to System Preferences in the Apple menu, then choose System. Scroll down to the Accessibility section and click on it. Press the VoiceOver button on the right to activate or deactivate VoiceOver.

Locate Specific Words By Hovering Over Them. Hold down the Command key while you move the cursor over the text; a window will pop up, displaying the text magnified.

Personalize The Hues Seen On Your Mac.
Color filter settings allow you to modify the display colors on your Mac. Select System Preferences from the Apple menu. In the System Preferences sidebar, pick Accessibility. On the right side, click Display to make the necessary changes. (If necessary, scroll below.) To easily distinguish between colors in the Accessibility Options, toggle this option on or off. You may access these settings by pressing Option-Command-F5, or by touching Touch ID three times in rapid succession on a Mac or Magic Keyboard with Touch ID.

Disabled Persons' Access To Audio

Immediately Add Captions. Captions for audio, video, and conversations may be added in real-time using Live Captions (beta). For more information on how to use Live Captions on macOS, see the User Guide.

Note: Not all languages, nations, or areas are supported by Live Captions at the moment since it is in beta. You shouldn't put your faith in Live Captions in critical or life-threatening circumstances since their accuracy could fluctuate.

Silence Distracting Sounds. Subdue distracting background noise by playing soothing noises, such as the beach or rain. Navigate to the Apple menu > System Settings, locate Accessibility in the sidebar, and finally, choose Audio. From there, you may enable Background noises. You may adjust the background sound's loudness by dragging the slider after selecting a sound effect from the available options.

Features That Facilitate Mobility Accessibility

Use Your Voice To Operate Your Mac. Voice Control allows you to do a lot of stuff just by speaking to it. Your personal information is safeguarded since all of the audio processing for Voice Control occurs on your Mac. Press Voice Control on the right side of the screen after clicking Accessibility in the sidebar after selecting Apple Menu > System Settings to enable Voice Control.

- Use your voice to type: Simply say "Dictation mode" to begin word-by-word dictation. Text is entered for any words said that aren't directives for voice control. Saying "Spelling mode" will also dictate each character.

- Use rich text editing to make rapid edits: swap out phrases, move the cursor to edit, and choose text with accuracy. "Say 'John just arrived' instead of 'John will be there soon.'" Suggested words and emojis make it easy to choose the one you want when you edit text.
- Voice commands may be used to access and interact with applications. Select items, scroll down, or click on them. Say "Show commands" to bring up the Commands box if you're not sure which commands you may use. If you want to see a label with a number next to each clickable object, you may say "show numbers" and then just mention the number you want to click. Saying "show grid" will overlay a grid on your screen, allowing you to click, zoom, drag, and more—even if you don't have control over that area of the screen.

For better word recognition by Voice Control, you may add custom terms and dictate custom spellings letter by letter. To add new vocabulary terms, go to System Settings > Accessibility, then choose Voice Control. After that, choose Vocabulary. When you're on the Voice Control options page, choose Commands. From there, you may customize the commands by adding new ones or keeping the default ones.

Make Your Pointer Unique. You may make the mouse pointer's form and outline more noticeable as it moves by using these settings.

Keyboard Accessibility Has Been Enhanced. With an extended range of keyboard shortcuts, you can manage your Mac with only the keyboard—no trackpad or mouse needed.

Enhancements To Speech Accessibility

Put Your Mac On Speaker Mode. If you want your text read aloud during a phone call, FaceTime chat, or in-person meeting, you may use Live Speech. Keep a list of often-used words so you can jump in when needed. A Personal Voice may be recorded or you can choose an existing voice to utilize.

HOW TO USE SCREEN TIME ON MACBOOK AIR

With Screen Time, you can see how much time you spend on your MacBook Air, find solutions to help you disconnect when you need a break, and keep tabs on your children's Apple device use.

Observe Your Macbook Air's Operation.
Learn which applications alert you the most, how often you use your smartphone daily, and how much time you spend on websites and apps by seeing reports for a day or a week. Start by opening System Settings. On the sidebar, pick Screen Time. Then, choose App & Website Activity, Notifications, or Pickups. These choices may not be visible until you enable Screen Time.

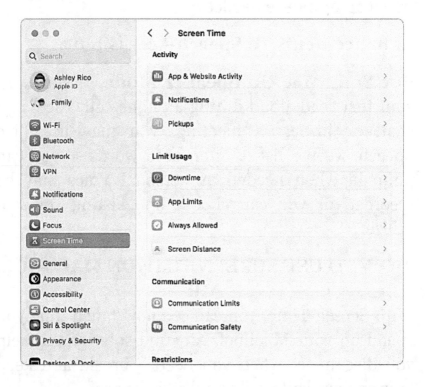

Establish Boundaries. Put time restrictions on individual applications, app categories, and websites to keep yourself in check. Select Downtime from Screen Time, toggle it on, and then use the pop-up menu to make a daily or weekly plan.

Reduce The Amount Of Time Your Children Spend In Front Of Screens. When parents set up Screen Time on their own Mac, iPhone, or iPad, their children's gadgets are prepared in the same way. Additionally, the Music and Book applications have the option to be rated according to age.

Keep In Mind What's Essential. You may set up automatic access to certain applications or websites. Select Always Allowed under Screen Time, and then enable the applications you want to keep open when you're not using them.

HOW TO CONNECT WITH OTHERS

Using FaceTime or another videoconferencing program on your MacBook Air, you may connect with people.

Make Use Of Facetime

Stay connected with anybody, anywhere with FaceTime. It works on any device, so you can have a conversation with just one person or a full group. Also, if you're connected to Wi-Fi, your MacBook

Air can make and receive calls. Moreover, you can send and receive text messages.

Get On Facetime. Make video calls with FaceTime on your Mac using the built-in FaceTime HD camera. After selecting New FaceTime, you may then input the contact's name, number, or email address before finally clicking FaceTime. If video calling isn't working for you, you may switch to audio-only calls by clicking the drop-down box and choosing FaceTime Audio. You have the option to join a FaceTime call with video or audio alone when you get the invitation.

For Group Chats, Try Using Facetime. A group call may have up to thirty-two participants. Collaborate with others by creating a one-of-a-kind connection. Link by clicking the "Create Link" button. Save the URL to your clipboard or send it to a friend via email or text message. A link is now available to join FaceTime calls from devices other than Apple.

Connect Your Phone To Facetime. To activate Wi-Fi calling on your iPhone (iOS 9 or later), go to Settings > Phone. So, launch FaceTime on your Mac. Find "Calls from iPhone" in the "General" section of Settings.

Make Use Of Messages And Facetime. To send and receive text messages on your MacBook Air, use Messages. Any time someone contacts you, you may react from any device—your MacBook Air, iPhone, iPad, iPod touch, or even your Apple Watch—because all messages are visible on all of these devices.

Enhance The Visual Experience Of Your Videoconference

When utilizing a video-capturing app like FaceTime with a suitable camera, you may improve your videoconferencing experience by choosing from a variety of video effects.

Take: Into consideration that the visual effects available to you can be limited to certain models of Macs or iPhones when utilizing them as webcams. The macOS User Guide has further information on how to use the video conferencing capabilities.

Make Your Video Better. Change the brightness, blur, and other video parameters to your liking. Select a camera mode (Portrait, Centre Stage, Studio Light, etc.) by clicking the Video button on the main menu.

Put The Mic In The Right Place. To switch between Voice Isolation and Wide Spectrum, go to the Video icon on the main menu and click on it.

Respond To The Discussion. Include an effect that causes the screen to be filled with entertaining 3D elements, such as fireworks, hearts, confetti, and more. After you've clicked the video icon on the menu bar, go to the Reactions menu and choose a response. Additionally, a simple hand gesture might convey your emotion. Verify the status of the green symbol next to Reactions, and observe See the FaceTime User Guide for a rundown of all the hand gestures you may use to respond during video effects in FaceTime chats.

Select The Screen You Want To Share With Ease. You may effortlessly share an app or many applications from the window you're currently in while on a chat with FaceTime or another compatible videoconferencing tool. While holding down the mouse button in the upper left corner of your screen, choose Mission Control. Then, choose Share on [your videoconferencing app name].

Superimpose Your Video On Top Of The Screen You've Shared. Big and little overlays are at your fingertips. One overlay puts you in a moveable bubble over your shared screen, drawing attention to you, while the other maintains you in the centre of attention with your screen framed next to you on a separate layer. Select Large or Small from the Presenter Overlay choice after clicking the Video symbol in the navigation bar.

Relate Stories With Shareplay

Listen to music, watch TV shows, or see material with your loved ones all at once with SharePlay. Anyone with an iOS 15 or later iPhone, iPad, or Mac running macOS Monterey or later may join in on the fun. Also, if you're using tvOS 15 or later, you can view content on Apple TV and have a conversation with pals on another device.

Keep: A subscription may be necessary to access some SharePlay-compatible applications. Some nations or areas may not have access to all features or material.

Jump Right Into Facetime. Launch FaceTime, invite your loved ones or coworkers, and then utilise the SharePlay icon to show them something. In Messages, you may also attach a SharePlay link to a post.

Join Me In Watching. Enjoy the company of others while viewing films of all kinds—movies, TV series, online videos, and more—in group FaceTime chats. The playback of all characters stays in sync regardless of whether you rewind, fast-forward, stop, or skip scenes. Smart volume allows you to keep chatting while viewing by automatically adjusting the volume.

We Should All Listen Attentively. Hold a mini-disco or full-on dance party by sharing music with your pals during FaceTime chats. During a group listening session, everyone may add music to a shared queue. You and your other callers may converse inaudibly thanks to the shared playback controls and smart volume.

Let Others See What's On Your Screen. Take advantage of SharePlay in FaceTime to include websites, applications, and more into your video chat. In a shared moment, whatever you see on your screen might be included. You may look at vacation rentals, find outfits for the bridesmaids, share a talent, or make a last-minute presentation in Photos. You may choose to share either one window or your whole screen.

HOW TO MANAGE WINDOWS ON YOUR MACBOOK AIR

When you have a dozen programmes active, each with its own window on your desktop, it's easy to feel overwhelmed. You can view and move around the open windows in a more efficient method, thankfully. When you need to concentrate, you may have one programme take up the whole screen or split the screen between two applications. Stage Manager will automatically arrange your windows and applications so that your desktop is clutter-free and you can navigate between activities with ease. Using Mission Control, you can organise all of your open windows into a one layer, making it easier to locate hidden windows. You may divide up your work among many computers and switch between them with ease by making use of multiple desktop areas.

Click to see window options.

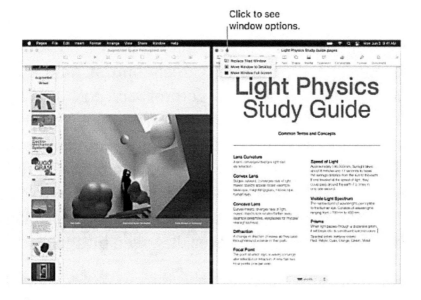

Make Full Use Of The Screen. In order to have your programme occupy the whole screen, you may use the full-screen view. You can use full-screen mode in a lot of Mac programmes, including Keynote, Numbers, and Pages. When you go to full screen, the menu bar doesn't appear until you hover your mouse over the top of the screen. However, you have the option to always display the menu bar as well. Navigate to the green button located in the upper left corner of the window. From the menu that displays, choose "Enter Full Screen" to activate or deactivate full-screen mode.

Divide The Display. If you want to use two apps simultaneously, you may use Split View. The two windows occupy the whole screen, much like full screen mode. Select the desired window by dragging the cursor to its top-left green button, and then select "Tile Window to Left of Screen" or "Tile Window to Right of Screen" from the resulting menu. As soon as you click on a different window, it will take up the opposite side of the screen. Options to switch programmes, bring both windows to full screen, and more appear in the menu that displays when the cursor hovers over the green button.

Managing The Stage. Keep your desktop free of clutter by automatically organising your programmes and windows. All of your other windows are conveniently located on the sides and can be accessed with a simple click, allowing you to keep your attention where it needs to be. To access the Stage Manager, open the Control Centre.

Control Room Mission. Consolidate all of your open windows into one layer with a simple click, and then bring up the current window in standard view. A row of spaces or applications in Split View will show up at the very top of the screen. Hit the Mission Control key (or the Control-Up Arrow) on the upper row of your keyboard to access or exit

Mission Control. You may also personalise your Dock by adding the Mission Control icon.

Application Components. In order to have quick access to your most used apps, you can add widgets from the widget gallery to your desktop. To edit widgets, add, delete, or rearrange them, click the date and time in the menu bar or Control-click the desktop. To add new widgets to your desktop or Notification Centre, just drag and drop them. You may also use your iPhone's widgets on your Mac's desktop without installing any programmes on your Mac if you're logged in with the same Apple ID on both devices.

Hint: You may swiftly shift any active windows to the side by clicking anywhere on the desktop background. This will allow you to see your desktop clearly even when you have numerous windows open. To return to your previous window, just click the desktop background once again.

When One Desktop Isn't Enough. Create several "desktop spaces" for your applications and move them around as needed. The Add Desktop button is located under Mission Control, therefore clicking it will create a new place. Navigate between areas with the help of Mission Control and keyboard shortcuts. Spaces may be added or removed as needed, and windows can be dragged from one to another.

That Traffic Signal That Is Horizontal. The three buttons—red, yellow, and green—located in the upper left corner of each window serve a purpose. To dismiss an app window, press the red button. This will exit the app and shut any windows that are associated with it, depending on the app. For others, it closes the current window but keeps the app open. The yellow button shuts the window momentarily and places it on the right side of the Dock. When you wish to reopen it, click it on the Dock to expand it. And the green button is an easy method to transform your windows to full screen and Split View, and more.

HOW TO TAKE SCREENSHOT ON YOUR MACBOOK AIR

If you want to know how to capture screenshots or record your screen, go into the Screenshot menu. While recording your screen, you may also record your voice. You may capture screen captures with the optimised workflow, and then modify, distribute, or save them with ease.

Get To The Controls For Taking Screenshots. Hit the Command-Shift-5 key. The screen as a whole, a specific window, or even just a region of the screen may be captured. You have the option to capture either the whole screen or a specific region.

The icons located at the bottom of the screen allow you to do a variety of tasks, such as recording your screen (Record Screen) and capturing a selection (Capture Screen Selection). Click Options to display the pointer, change the save location, alter the microphone and audio settings, or to set a timeout before capturing. Press the Record or Capture button to start recording.

In the bottom right corner of your screen, you'll see a thumbnail that shows when you capture a video or screenshot. Quickly save by swiping to the right, modify or share by clicking, or drag the thumbnail into a folder.

Note: To use the Screenshot tool, you may use Launchpad's Other folder or go to the Finder's Apps > Utilities folder.

Annotate Your Screen Capture. To use the Markup tools and annotate your screenshot, click on its thumbnail. You can also share your annotated screen with friends and coworkers by clicking the share button inside the screenshot.

HOW TO TRANSFER YOUR DATA TO YOUR NEW MACBOOK AIR

You may move your data and settings from another Mac or PC to your new MacBook Air. When you boot up your brand new MacBook Air for the first time, you'll be asked whether you would want to import data from another device. Please choose an option below if you would like to immediately begin transferring data from your new computer.

Before You Begin

- Be sure to install the most recent operating system updates on your old and new computers before you start. Select your current operating system from the menu at the top of the page to get the most precise instructions.
- Make sure both devices are on the same network in order to wirelessly transmit data.

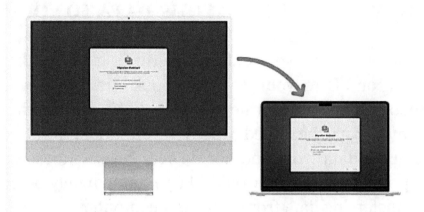

Data Transfer From A Different Mac

If you have an Ethernet connection between your old and new machines, or if you're using a wireless network, you may use Migration Assistant to move your data. To install Migration Assistant on both Macs, launch Finder, go to Applications, open the Utilities folder, double-click Migration Assistant, and then observe the onscreen prompts. During a wireless transmission, it is best to maintain the computers in close proximity to one another.

Move Files From A Computer

Any data, whether wireless or wired, may be transferred with the help of Windows Migration Assistant. Please refer to the Apple Support page titled "Transfer from PC to Mac with Migration

Assistant" for information on how to determine whether version of Migration Assistant is compatible with your Windows PC.

Move Files Across Storage Devices

See MacBook Air Adapters for information on how to connect the storage device to your laptop.

Get Your Files Transferred From A Time Machine Archive.

With Migration Assistant, you may easily recover data from a Time Machine backup in the event that your prior computer's hard disc had data corruption.

HOW TO BACKUP AND RESTORE YOUR MACBOOK AIR

The data stored on your MacBook Air should be backed up on a regular basis. If you want to protect your Mac's programmes, accounts, settings, media, documents, and images, you may use the built-in Time Machine. You can't use Time Machine to create a backup of macOS.

You Must Choose A Location To Store Your Backup Data. When you use Time Machine to back up your MacBook Air, it can use any supported storage device, including external drives.

Launch Time Machine. Make sure your MacBook Air and the external storage device are on the same Wi-Fi network, or use the appropriate adapter to connect the two devices via cable. Before you start, check the instructions that came with your storage device. For more information, see Adapters for your MacBook Air. Launch System Preferences, go to General > Time Machine, and finally, choose Add Backup Disc. Just choose the disc you want to use for backups, and you're good to go.

Get Your Files Back. You have the option to restore certain files or all of them simultaneously when you use Time Machine to back up your data. Go to the menu bar, find the Time Machine icon, and choose "Browse Time Machine backups." You may restore only certain folders or the whole disc; just choose what you need to restore and hit the restore button.

Keep in mind that you may access Control Centre in the sidebar of your Mac from the Apple Menu (System Settings) if you can't see the Time Machine symbol in the menu bar. To display Time Machine in the menu bar, click the pop-up menu next to it on the right.

Set Up MacOS Again. Separate from your personal information, your operating system files are stored on a sealed system disc. But if you delete or accidentally damage a disc, for example, you'll need to restore your MacBook Air. Restoring your personal data from a backup using Time Machine is an option after reinstalling macOS. Multiple methods exist for restoring your Mac with macOS Big Sur and subsequent versions. A more recent version of macOS than the one that came with your machine or the one you were using prior to the disc damage may be necessary for installation.

Note: Power users may choose to build a bootable installer for future macOS reinstallations. If there's a particular macOS version you'd want to utilise, this may be helpful.

HOW TO SHARE CONTENT BETWEEN DEVICES

Sharing media across Apple devices is easy in many ways. Copy and paste text, images, and passwords across devices using Universal Clipboard or use AirDrop to send and receive files.

Using Airdrop, You May Share Files And More

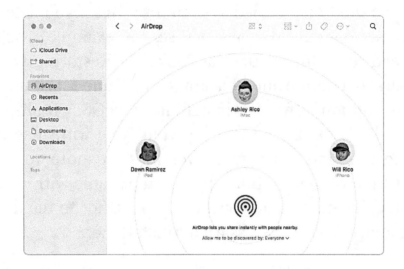

Through the use of AirDrop, it is simple to transfer files between neighbouring iOS devices. No Apple ID is required for the devices to work together.

Toggle Airdrop On. To access Control Centre, go to the menu bar and look for the symbol for AirDrop. Make sure only those you're already in contact with may AirDrop files to you by selecting "Contacts only".

Get A File Out Of Finder And Send It. To transmit an item to another device, control-click it, then pick Share > AirDrop. After that, choose the device you want to send it to. Alternately, you may access AirDrop from the Dock's Finder icon by selecting it (or by going to Go > AirDrop). From the desktop or another Finder window, drag the file to the recipient when their name displays in the window. The receiver of a file has the option to accept or reject it when you transmit it to them.

Share A File Via A Mobile App. Click the Share option in Pages or Preview, then pick AirDrop. Then, choose the device you want to send the item to.

Advice: Check that both devices are within 30 feet (9 metres) of each other and that AirDrop and Bluetooth are enabled if the receiver is not visible in the AirDrop window. Select "Don't see who you're looking for?" if you think the receiver is on a more ancient Mac.

Send And Receive Files Using Airdrop. You have the option to accept or store files sent to your Mac by others via AirDrop. You can save files via AirDrop to your Downloads folder or an app like Photos after you click Accept when you wish to receive them. Using the same iCloud account across several devices makes it easy to transfer and store media files (such an iPhone picture) from one device to another.

HOW TO USE HANDOFF ON YOUR MACBOOK AIR

Click to continue what you were doing on your iPhone.

When you're using Handoff, you may pick up just where you left off on another device. The next time you're away from your work, start a FaceTime call on your iPhone and transfer it to your MacBook Air. For example, you may start a presentation on your MacBook Air and finish it off on your iPad. Read a message on your wrist and reply on your laptop. Handoff is compatible with Keynote, Pages, FaceTime, Safari, Mail, Calendar, Contacts, Maps, Messages, Reminders, and Keynote.

Transfer Control From One Device To Another. When your MacBook Air and another device are in close proximity to one other, you'll usually see an indicator in the Dock that indicates when you may pass an activity on. To switch between devices, just click the symbol.

The FaceTime handoff icon is missing from the Dock. Instead, in the FaceTime window on your Mac, you may transfer a call from your iOS device to your MacBook Air by clicking the video symbol in the menu bar, then selecting Switch. Once you're on FaceTime with your MacBook Air, you may transfer the call to your iOS device by tapping the video symbol on the top left of your iOS device, then tapping Switch.

For Your MacBook Air, Activate Handoff. Select "Allow Handoff between this Mac and your iCloud devices." After opening System Settings, click General in the sidebar. Then, click Airdrop & Handoff.

Your iOS Or ipadOS Device Has To Have Handoff Turned On. You may enable Handoff by going to Settings > General > Handoff and tapping on it. Your gadget doesn't have Handoff capability if you can't see the choice.

Get Your Apple Watch Ready For Handoff Mode. You may enable handoff in the Apple Watch app on an iPhone by going to Settings > General and tapping the corresponding button.

Transfer Files From One Device To Another

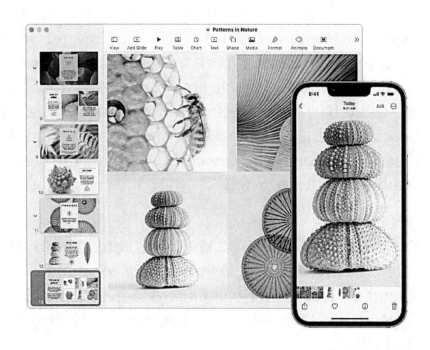

Rapidly copy and paste material from one device to another in close proximity. When you use the same Apple ID across all of your iOS devices—Macs, iPhones, iPads, and iPod touches—and enable Handoff, Wi-Fi, and Bluetooth, the contents of your Clipboard are transferred over Wi-Fi and made accessible to all of those devices.

Transfer Data Across Files. With Universal Clipboard, copying and pasting across Macs is a breeze. You may copy and paste files on your MacBook Air into Finder, Mail, or any programme that supports the feature. On both devices, you need to have your Apple ID shown.

Transfer Images From Your iPhone To Your Mac

With Continuity Camera for Mac, you can connect your iPhone to your Mac and use it as an extra camera. Take pictures with your iPhone's camera and then either add them to your papers or transfer them to your Mac.

Make A Scan Or Insert A Picture. Scan papers or snap a photo of an object in your immediate vicinity using the camera on your iOS device. On your Mac, the picture is immediately visible. Once you've decided where you want the picture to appear in an app like Messages, Mail, or Notes, click File (or Insert) > Import From iPhone or iPad. Then, pick Take Photo or Scan Documents. Finally, use your iOS or iPadOS device to take the photo or scan the image. Select either Keep Scan or Use Photo. To try again, just hit the Retake button.

Once you've decided where to put the picture in an app like Pages, all you have to do is control-click, pick "Import image," and snap the shot. Choosing your device before snapping a picture may be necessary.

Important: If you're using an iOS or iPadOS device, you may take a scan by dragging the frame till you see what you want to capture, then tapping Keep Scan and finally tapping Save. To scan the material again, tap Retake.

You may position the image or scan wherever you want in the paper.

HOW TO STREAM CONTENT ON A LARGER SCREEN WITH AIRPLAY

If you have a MacBook Air and want to show off what's on it on a larger screen, you can use AirPlay to transfer media from your iOS device to your Mac. If you have a high-resolution TV, you can either utilise it as an additional display or mirror the MacBook Air screen onto it. Make sure your MacBook Air and Apple TV are both connected to the same Wi-Fi network, and then hook up your TV to Apple TV. When you want to watch a movie but don't want others to see what you're working on, you may play online films straight on your high-definition TV without revealing your desktop.

Access Media On Your Mac From A Variety Of Devices. Stream media from your Mac to all of your other devices at the same time. In programmes like Keynote and Photos, which enable it, you may mirror your iOS device's screen onto your Mac, or you can use your Mac as an additional display to expand the screen of your iOS device. If you have an AirPlay 2 speaker, you can listen to podcasts and music directly on your Mac, or you may utilise it as an additional speaker in a multiroom setup. Any Apple device may be used with your Mac, and it's much simpler to connect when the devices use the same Apple ID.

Screen Mirroring Allows You To Reflect Your Desktop. Select your Apple TV by clicking the Control Centre symbol in the menu bar, then select Screen Mirroring. You can tell AirPlay is on when the icon changes to blue.

Note: When an Apple TV is connected to the same network as your Mac, you will see an AirPlay status symbol in the menu bar if your Mac supports screen mirroring using AirPlay. Refer to the macOS User Guide for information on how to use AirPlay to stream media from your Mac.

View Online Videos In A Desktop-Hidden Format. To play a web video on your Apple TV, just look for the AirPlay symbol and click on it.

You may purchase Apple TV on its own from apple.com or any Apple Store in your neighbourhood.

Hint: change the desktop size to get the best picture if mirroring the screen doesn't work on your high-resolution TV. To adjust the video's aspect ratio to your desktop, find the AirPlay symbol inside the player and click on it.

HOW TO WORK WITH MULTIPLE DEVICES

Your Mac is compatible with all of your other Apple products. When you utilise your Mac, iPad, iPhone, or Apple Watch with Continuity, you have access to amazing features.

Prior to starting. Turn on Wi-Fi and Bluetooth on both your MacBook Air and iOS or iPadOS device. Make sure you're logged in with the same Apple ID.

Make Use Of Your Mac And iPhone

Transform Your Desktop With iPhone Widgets. Easily add widgets from your iPhone to your Mac desktop. Drag and drag widgets from Notification Centre onto your desktop or use the Widget Gallery to choose iPhone widgets for your Mac. Just right-click the desktop and choose "Edit Widgets" to access the Widget Gallery.

The iPhone May Be Used As A Webcam. With Continuity Camera for Mac, you can connect your iPhone to your Mac and use it as an extra camera. A video call may be made using the camera of an iPhone. Once Continuity Camera is configured, your Mac will be able to detect when your iPhone is nearby and instantly switch to utilising it as a camera. A wired connection is also an option for you to consider.

Note: The Continuity Camera cannot be used as a webcam unless you own an iPhone XR or a later model. Continuity Camera requires iOS 12 or later on iPhones and iPod touches or iPadOS 13.1 or later on iPads in order to exchange photographs.

Tap On The Microphone On Your iPhone. Continuity Camera allows you to connect your iPhone to your Mac and use it as a microphone. You may choose your iPhone to use for a video call from the Video option in FaceTime, or you can change the app's settings to utilise your iPhone's microphone. Another option is to go into System Preferences > Audio and then choose your iPhone to use as the system microphone.

Connect Your iPhone To Your Mac. You may use many of the same applications on your Mac that you can on your iPhone or iPad.

Mac For Phone Conversations And Texting. You may make and receive calls on your MacBook Air using a Wi-Fi connection. Moreover, you are able to send and receive text messages.

Wi-Fi calling may be enabled on an iPhone by going to Settings > Phone. So, launch FaceTime on your Mac. Find "Calls from iPhone" in the "General" section of Settings.

You May Use Your iPhone To Create A Wireless Hotspot. Is your Wi-Fi no longer working? In a flash, your MacBook Air may join the internet over your iOS device's Personal Hotspot— no password needed—thanks to Instant Hotspot.

To access your iOS device's network settings, go to the menu bar, find the Wi-Fi status icon, and then, in the list of available networks, choose the Links icon. If you don't see the list, choose Other Networks. In the toolbar, the Wi-Fi symbol transforms into the Links icon. The MacBook Air immediately connects, so there's no need to do anything on your end. Your MacBook Air power saver automatically disconnects from the hotspot when it detects that you aren't using it.

Advice: Verify that all of your devices are in the right configuration if you are prompted for a password. Refer to the article on Apple Support. Quickly connect to your Personal Hotspot without having to input a password by using Instant Hotspot.

Get The Most Out Of Your iPad And Mac

Pairing your MacBook Air with an iPad will maximise its potential. Sidecar allows you to utilise your iPad as an additional display for your Mac, providing you with more room to spread out your work and use the Apple Pencil in your preferred Mac applications. The ability to utilise your Mac's keyboard, mouse, and trackpad to manage your iPad is known as Universal manage, and it facilitates the transfer of media between the two operating systems. In addition, you may annotate PDFs, screenshots, and more with ease.

Transform Your Ipad Into An Extra Monitor For Your Mac. Use your iPad wirelessly within ten metres (32 feet) of your Mac using Sidecar, or charge it by connecting it to your Mac via cable. Navigate to the Apple menu > System Settings, then click Displays. From the Add Display pop-up menu, choose your iPad to set it up as a second display. In Control Center's Display section, you'll find the option to connect to your iPad later on. To detach your iPad from your Mac, go Control Centre and look for the Sidecar button. Another option is to use the iPad's sidebar, where you should see the Disconnect icon.

Sidecar is compatible with iPads running iPadOS 13.1 or later and devices that support the Apple Pencil.

Set Sidecar Setting. Go to your iPad's name in the list of devices in System Settings, then choose Displays. You may then customise your iPad's Sidecar settings, such as its primary display, whether it mirrors your Mac, the visibility and placement of the sidebar, and the ability to double-tap with the Apple Pencil to access features.

Note: These choices will not be shown in the Display settings of an iPad that has not been configured.

Take Use Of The Apple Pencil. Get professional results with your favourite drawing and editing programmes. To begin using Apple Pencil on your iPad, just move the window from your Mac to the tablet. Alternatively, an Apple Pencil may be used to annotate photos, screenshots, and PDFs.

Note: In order for the pressure and tilt features of the Apple Pencil to function, the applications in question must have advanced silhouette support.

Mirror Or Extend Your Desktop. By connecting your iPad to your Mac, it will appear as an extra desktop for your Mac, allowing you to easily move programmes and data between the two devices. By dragging the mouse pointer over the Sidecar button, you may mirror the display of your Mac on both devices. Select Mirror Built-in Retina Display from the Sidecar menu button in Control Centre by clicking the right arrow that appears above the button. Select Use As Separate Display from the options to resize your desktop.

Use The Quick Links On The Sidebar. To get to the controls and buttons you use most often, utilise the iPad's sidebar. Use the buttons to reverse activities, access keyboard shortcuts, and show or conceal the Dock, keyboard, and menu bar.

Hint: If you want the Sidecar settings to be shown in the menu bar at all times, you may change the Display settings to that. To toggle the visibility of the Displays icon in the menu bar, go to System

Settings > Control Centre. From the pop-up menu next to Displays, choose either Always or Only when active. Sidecar transforms the Display icon in the menu bar into the Sidecar menu button when your iPad is connected and Sidecar is enabled.

Manage Several Devices With Only One Set Of Input Devices—A Keyboard, A Mouse, And A Trackpad. One set of input devices—a keyboard, a mouse, and a trackpad—can manage all of your connected devices with Universal Control. By dragging the cursor to the edge of your MacBook Air screen, you can easily switch between your iPad and another Mac, allowing you to work seamlessly across up to three devices.

Note: You'll need macOS 12.3 or later on your Mac and iPadOS 15.4 or later on your iPad to make use of Universal Control.

Verify Your Links. In order to pair with additional devices, Universal Control on Mac employs Bluetooth and Wi-Fi. Make sure that all of your devices are connected to Wi-Fi and that Bluetooth is enabled. On both the MacBook Air and the iPad, go to Settings > General > AirPlay & Handoff and toggle Handoff on. In addition to having two-factor authentication enabled, you need to be logged in with the same Apple ID on both gadgets. You may use Control Centre to link your devices once these settings are accurate. Select a device from the list that appears underneath Link Keyboard and Mouse in Mac's Control Centre. Then, pick Screen Mirroring from the menu bar.

Switch Between Displays. When using a Mac, go to the screen's edge that is nearest to your iPad (either the right or left side), press and hold to stop, and then drag the pointer just beyond the screen's edge. Keep dragging the cursor to the edge of the iPad screen until you see a boundary.

Drag And Drop. You may transfer text, images, or other objects from one device to another simply by selecting them and dragging them to the desired location. As an example, you can transfer an Apple Pencil drawing from your iPad to your MacBook

Air's Keynote programme. Additionally, you may copy text from one device and paste it onto another.

Share A Keyboard. Start typing as soon as the insertion point starts flashing in a document or any other place where text may be entered.

HOW TO USE MACBOOK AIR APPS

THE APP STORE

Find and install applications, as well as see when they've been updated, by searching the App Store.

Discover The Ideal App. Confident in your search criteria? To search for an app, type its name into the box and hit Return. When you install an app from the App Store, Launchpad will instantly display it. Alternately, you may peruse the results for new applications by selecting a tab from the sidebar, such as Create, Work, or Play.

Click a tab to browse apps.

Search for an app by name.

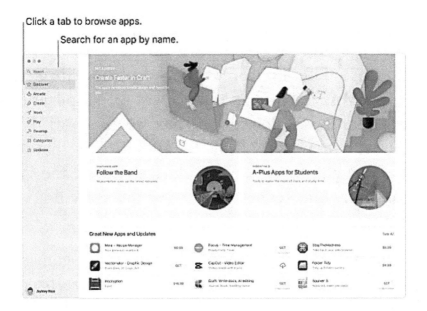

Note: Not everywhere you look you can find Apple Arcade.

Just ask Siri. "Look for applications that children can use."

Just An Apple ID Is Required. To access the App Store and download free applications, sign in using your Apple ID. You can find the Sign In button at the bottom of the sidebar. Click Sign In, and then choose Create Apple ID if you haven't already. Click "Forgot Apple ID or password?" to retrieve your forgotten password if you have an Apple ID but can't recall it. To purchase applications that cost money, you'll also need to create an account and provide payment details.

Harness The Power Of iOS Applications On Your Mac. You can use a lot of applications designed for iOS devices on your MacBook Air. Your Mac will show you all of the applications that you have bought for your iOS device. Check the App Store for Mac compatibility while searching for software.

Game On. To access Apple Arcade, select games to play, check which titles your Game Centre friends have recommended, track your accomplishment progress, and more, go to the Arcade tab. Whether you're using a controller or not, all of your downloaded games from the App Store will be conveniently located under the Games folder in Launchpad.

Game Mode. Game Mode reduces background task utilisation by automatically giving games first priority on your Mac's CPU and GPU when you play a game. When used with wireless devices, such as AirPods and your preferred controllers, it significantly decreases latency, allowing you to experience responsiveness firsthand.

Make A Copy Of Your Current Game Progress. For the purpose of reviewing your game strategy or recording unforgettable gaming moments, you may record up to a fifteen-second video clip of gameplay by hitting the share button on compatible third-party game controllers.

Share The Game With Your Friends. Invite your recent Messages friends and groups to play games that are compatible with Game Centre using the new multiplayer friend option. Check the friend request inbox for any invites or requests that may arrive.

Keep Current With The Newest App Versions. The presence of a badge on the Dock icon representing the App Store indicates that there are available updates. Launch the App Store by clicking the icon; then, on the sidebar, choose Updates.

You have
available updates.

THE CALENDAR

Make sure you never miss a meeting by using Calendar. Make use of many calendars and manage them from a single location to keep track of your hectic schedule.

Design Occasions. You may add additional events by clicking the Add button or by double-clicking on any day. To add a new event fast, you may also utilise Spotlight. Just double-click the event, go to the Add Invitees area, and enter an email address to invite someone. The calendar will notify you when the invitees respond.

Just ask Siri. For example, you may say, "Please arrange a meeting with Mark for the morning at nine o'clock."

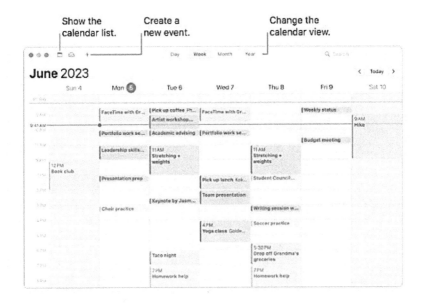

Show the calendar list.

Create a new event.

Change the calendar view.

Hint: Calendar displays a map, estimated journey time, departure time, and weather prediction when you include a place with an event.

Every Aspect Of Your Life May Be Marked On A Calendar. Make three coloured calendars: one for your house, one for your office, and one for your classroom. After you've made a calendar by selecting File > New Calendar, you may change its colour by Control-clicking on each calendar individually.

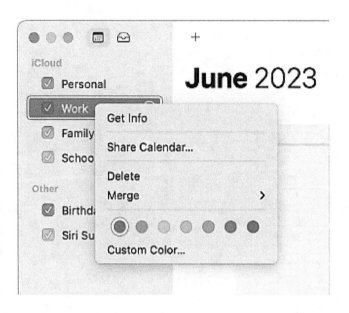

Insert Calendars For Holidays. Check out the holiday schedules for various countries and areas. Select a holiday calendar to add by going to File > New Holiday Calendar.

View Every One Of Your Calendars, Or Choose A Few. Select the calendars you want to see in the window by clicking on them from the list that appears when you click the Calendars button.

Focus Is A Calendar Filter. Pick the calendars you want to display when a certain Focus is active. Take a study-only calendar as an example; it will only turn on while you are actively working on an assignment. Select Focus from the sidebar after going to System Preferences in the Apple Menu. Click the right arrow after you've picked a focus on the right, then go to the Focus Filters menu and select Add Filter.

Use It On All Of Your Devices And Share It With Others. All of your calendars on all of your iOS devices, Macs, Apple Watches, and iPads powered by iOS and signed in with the same Apple ID are automatically synced when you login in to iCloud. Other iCloud users may also see your calendars.

THE MESSAGES

No matter what device you're using, staying in contact is simple with Messages. Enjoy a plethora of features, such as managing group messages, quickly accessing material shared with you, and more. If you have an iOS device—a Mac, iPhone, iPad, iPod touch, or Apple Watch—you can use iMessage to text other people, and if you don't, you can use SMS or MMS.

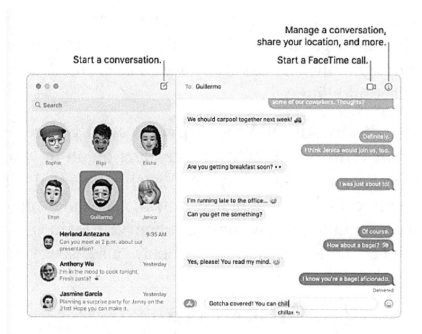

Start a conversation.

Manage a conversation, share your location, and more.

Start a FaceTime call.

Your iMessage Message Limit Is Unlimited.
By logging in with your Apple ID, you have limitless messaging capabilities with everyone who also has a Mac, iPhone, iPad, iPod touch, or Apple Watch. This includes text, images, Live images, video, and more. Messages sent to these devices are encrypted and shown in blue bubbles inside your chats in the Messages app. The macOS User Guide provides instructions on how to set up messages on a Mac.

Dial The Number. If you have an iPhone running iOS 8.1 or later and have logged in to Messages with the same Apple ID as your Mac, you may send and receive SMS and MMS messages on your Mac even if you're not using iMessage. Text Message Forwarding may be enabled on an iPhone by going to Settings > Messages, tapping Text Message Forwarding, and finally tapping the name of your Mac. If your Apple ID does not use two-factor authentication, you will receive an activation code on your Mac. On your iPhone, input the code and then press Allow. Your unencrypted text messages (SMS and MMS) will show up in green bubbles during chats.

Just ask Siri. Just let Mom know that you'll be late.

You Can Modify And Unsend Messages. You have two minutes from the moment you send a message to unsend it or make five edits to it within fifteen minutes of sending it. This is all part of the Messages feature. To undo or edit a sent message, just control-click on it.

"Mark As Unread" A Discussion. To come back to an unread message when you have a moment to react, you may mark it as unread. To mark a message as unread, control-click on it in the list of messages.

Prioritise Interactions You Like. Move the discussions you want to keep at the forefront of your messages list by dragging and dropping them. Above a pinned discussion, you'll see new messages, Tapbacks, and typing indications. In a group chat, the most current members show up around the pinned discussion while there are unread messages.

Oversee Discussions Within A Group. You may make a group more noticeable by using an emoji, picture, or Memoji as their image. By entering the person's name or swiping right on any message in a group chat, you may direct a message to that person. To react to a question or statement that was already made, you can add your response as an inline reply. When a discussion becomes too lively, you have the option to hide chat notifications. Once you've chosen a discussion from the list, you can access its management settings and configure the group picture by clicking the Details button in the top-right corner of the Messages window. Go to Messages > Settings, choose General, and then select the "Notify me when my name is mentioned" option to get a notice whenever your name is mentioned.

Add Some Humour To Your Communications. Make conversations more interesting by adding stickers, Tapbacks, popular GIFs, or unique effects like balloons, fluttering confetti, or more to your replies. If you make a sticker on your iPhone and then sync it with iCloud, you can access it on any of your iOS devices, including your iPad and Mac. Pick out a sticker that sums up your feelings, then add it to a discussion by clicking the Apps icon, then selecting Stickers. To add a sticker to a particular message in a chat, you may simply drag & drop. Press and hold a message to add a Tapback, such a thumbs up or thumbs down. Select #images or Message Effects from the Apps menu, and then select the desired GIF or special effect to add. Keep an eye out for your friends' handwritten notes sent to you from their iPhone, iPad, or Apple Watch, as well as Digital Touch and invisible ink.

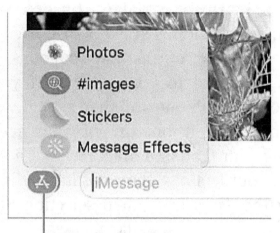

Add a photo, sticker, video, or effect.

Make A Unique Memoji. Personalise your very own Memoji by selecting their skin tone, freckles, hair colour, facial characteristics, and more. Navigate to Messages > Settings to set a customised Memoji as your Messages profile picture. Press Continue after selecting "Set up Name and Photo Sharing," and then choose Customise. After you've clicked the New Memoji button, you may customise your appearance by clicking on each feature. To complete adding the Memoji sticker to your collection, click Done. Have fun creating new Memojis by opening a discussion, going to the Apps menu, selecting Stickers, and finally, clicking the New Memoji button.

Transmit An Image, Movie, Or File. Simply drag and drop files into Messages to share them. Alternatively, you may import media from your Photos collection and email them out in no time. You may add a picture to a discussion by clicking the Apps icon, then Photos. To narrow your search for a particular picture, you may include keywords like a person's name, a date, or a place.

Simple Picture Administration. If someone gives you a bunch of images, you could see a collage of two or three of them at a glance, or a stack of four or more. You may see each picture in the stack without opening them by swiping left or right with two fingers on a trackpad or Magic Mouse. To open, respond to, or add a Tapback to an image, just control-click on it. Pressing the Save Photo button next to an image allows you to swiftly save it to Photos. When you double-click the stack, all of the images therein will be opened.

Look For The Correct Message. By combining search criteria, you may swiftly restrict your search and find the message you need. You may see your results organised by category, including discussions, messages, and photographs, and you can quickly search your conversations by multiple parameters, like person or keyword.

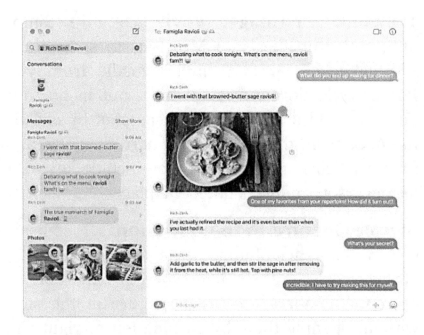

The Shared With You Search Interface, As Seen In The Messages Pane. The Messages content that your Contacts send you will be saved in the app's new Shared with You area, so you can access it whenever it's convenient for you. Photographs, Safari, Apple News, Apple Podcasts, and the Apple TV app all display material that has been shared with you. You can see the sender of shared material in the relevant applications and quickly launch the accompanying discussion in Messages with a click. This way, you can continue the conversation while enjoying the shared content.

Tip: By clicking the Details icon, you may see all of the photographs included in a chat.

Work Together On Tasks. A wide variety of file formats, including Keynote presentations, spreadsheets in Numbers, documents in Pages, notes, and more, may be shared by invitation. To begin collaborating in an app, go to the Share menu, choose Collaborate, and finally, hit the Messages button. Everyone in the thread will be instantly added to the shared document, spreadsheet, or other file when you choose the name of the group you wish to include as participants. At the very top of the Messages thread, you may observe activity updates whenever someone makes an alteration.

Let Others See What's On Your Screen. By dragging and dropping files on the shared desktop, you and your buddy may access folders, create documents, and share screens. To access the screen sharing options, first select the Details icon.

Join Us In Watching And Listening. You may watch and listen to a SharePlay session on your Mac by joining it using Messages. Even when on a FaceTime conversation, you may share what's on your screen.

Note: A subscription may be necessary to access some SharePlay-compatible applications. Some nations or areas may not have access to all features or material.

Use Focus To Sort Your Messages. During each Focus, you may choose see the messages you're interested in. For a Gaming Focus, for instance, all you have to do is listen in on chats with your normal gaming pals. Select Focus from the sidebar after going to System Preferences in the Apple Menu. Click the right arrow after you've picked a focus on the right, then go to the Focus Filters menu and select Add Filter.

THE IMOVIE

With iMovie, you can easily edit your home films into professional-looking movies and trailers, and then share them with the world.

Bring In A Movie. Quickly and easily import video from your iOS device, camera, or other media files on your Mac. A new library and event are automatically created by iMovie.

View your
projects.

Correct and adjust
color in your clip.

Share a movie,
trailer, or clip.

Use The Integrated Camera To Capture Video. Record video with your Mac's FaceTime HD camera and include it into your project. Pick an event from the sidebar, go to the toolbar and click Import. Then, choose FaceTime HD Camera. Finally, press the Record button to begin and stop recording.

Design Trailers In The Manner Of Hollywood. Create ingenious trailers with soaring tunes and dynamic visuals. To make your own, all you have to do is add some media and change the credits. First, go to the New button. Then, choose Trailer. In the Trailer box, pick a template. Finally, click Create. In the Outline tab, you may enter the names of the actors and crew, and in the Storyboard page, you can include your own media.

Click Play to preview the trailer.

Hint: If you're using a handheld camera, you can stabilise the footage to make it play back more smoothly. If the video is shaky, select it in the timeline, and then go to the Stabilisation menu and choose Stabilise Shaky Video.

THE KEYNOTE

Make state-of-the-art presentations like an expert using Keynote. Pick one of the thirty+ premade themes and personalise it with your own text, 3D objects, and colour scheme. Collaborating on a

Keynote presentation while keeping track of any changes is now simpler than ever using Activity Stream.

Use Visuals To Organise. To easily insert, reorder, or remove slides, use the left-hand slide navigator. To see a slide in the main window, click on it. To rearrange their order, just drag them. To delete a slide, pick it and hit the Delete button.

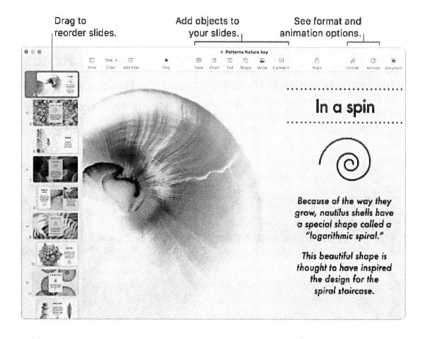

Work Together Via Messages. Anyone participating in a conversation in Messages will be instantly invited to the Keynote presentation when you send out a collaboration invitation. Select

Collaborate from the drop-down menu, then click the Share icon. From there, choose Messages. Pick the organisation whose members you would want to include.

Collaborate Instantly. Anyone working on a Keynote presentation with you may view their modifications and comments in Activity Stream's comprehensive sidebar list. Everyone's edits, even those to the Keynote presentation or other files, are easily trackable.

Execution Is The Key. Select Play > Rehearse Slideshow to practise your presentation. You can see your notes on each slide and a clock to help you stay on schedule.

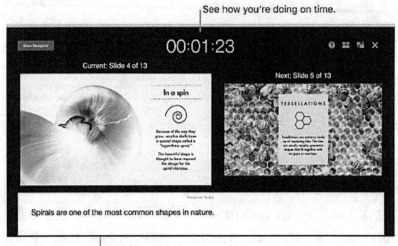

Regardless Of The Circumstance. Use your Mac to see forthcoming slides, presenter notes, a clock, and a timer while presenting in person using an external monitor. You may manage a slideshow just as you would while presenting alone during a videoconference. Make a presentation that the audience can engage with; use your iOS device (iPhone, iPad, or Apple Watch) to manage the presentation from anywhere; and much more besides.

Hand Over The Slideshow. Select Share > Send a Copy to send a copy via Mail, Messages, AirDrop, or even social media if you would want your boss to evaluate your presentation or if you would like to share it with others on a conference call.

Captivate Them. Use the slide's animation features to grab their attention. After selecting the object, go to the toolbar and click on Animate. In the sidebar, click on Action. Finally, click on Add an Effect.

Advice: Think about adding a video to your presentation. Once you've decided where to put it, go to the toolbar and find the Media button. After selecting "Photos or Videos," choose the desired video and drop it into your presentation slide.

THE MAPS

See where you are and how to get there with the help of a map or satellite picture. With Apple's selected city guides, you can find out what the top attractions are. To place a pin in a specific spot, use the Force button.

Look Into It Thoroughly. Discover more about the world around you with the assistance of maps that display additional data like landmarks, elevation, and natural features. Experience fresh cityscapes on your Mac with Apple silicon, complete with trees, landmarks, and buildings.

Find A Path. Plan your route, see road features (such as turn and bus lanes), and monitor traffic using the new driving map. Make it easy to see your multi-stop route plans on your iPhone or send them to a friend in a flash using Messages.

Save The Ones You Like The Most. Sort the results according to your criteria. Find out crucial details about an establishment, such its hours of operation or if it provides takeaway, by clicking on it. The locations you visit the most might be marked as favourites.

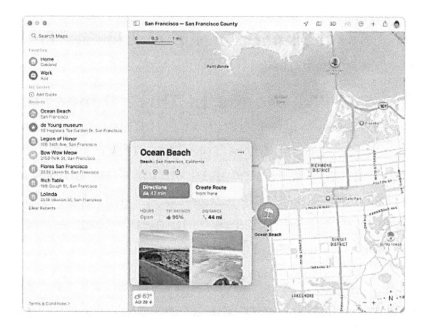

Just Ask Siri. Just say, "Find coffee near me."

Guides May Help You Discover New Locations. Trusted companies and partners produce Maps' curated recommendations to help you find amazing places to eat, shop, and explore across the globe. When new locations are added, you may bookmark these directions and get updates.

Make Your Very Own Manuals. Make personalised itineraries for the locations you love and show them off to your loved ones. To begin making a guide, hover your mouse over My Guides in the sidebar, then click the Add icon on the right. To access the settings menu, control-click on the newly-created guide.

Feel Free To Explore In Three Dimensions. Explore some cities in 3D while gliding fluidly over the streets in an interactive experience by clicking the Look Around binoculars button. The interactive 3D Globe is available on Macs powered by Apple hardware, allowing users to immerse themselves in the Earth's natural splendour.

For Important Locations, Refer To The Indoor Maps. Learn the layout of certain airports and retail centres. Discover nearby eateries, locate restrooms, plot a meeting point at the mall, and much more with just a little zooming in.

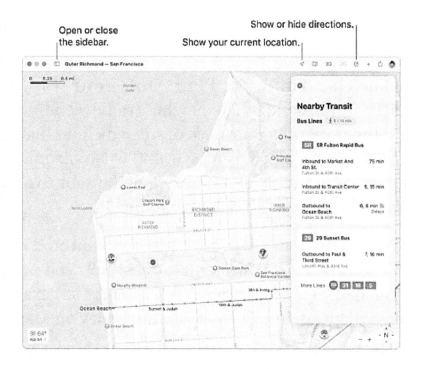

Open or close the sidebar.

Show your current location.

Show or hide directions.

Ride The Bus Or Train There. You may see future departures near you and other Nearby Transit information for selected cities on Maps. To see potential routes, prices, and times for using public transport, just click on a location in the sidebar and then the transit symbol. Make sure your preferred tube lines are always front and centre when you're near them by pinning them.

Easy EV Travel Planning Made Simple. You may connect your EV to your iPhone and use Maps to find charging stations along the way. It will also factor in the time it takes to charge when estimating your arrival time.

Take The Time To Plan Out Your Bicycle Path. Information like height, traffic conditions, and the presence or absence of steep inclines may be seen on maps, which can be useful when planning a bicycle journey. Your itinerary may be sent to your iPhone after you've finished planning it.

Verify The Most Up-To-Date Estimated Time Of Arrival. If your loved ones tell you their estimated time of arrival (ETA), you may see exactly where they are in relation to their journey on Maps.

Note: There are certain nations or locations that do not have access to certain Maps features.

Warning: See crucial safety information for your Mac for crucial details regarding navigation and avoiding distractions that might put you in danger.

Hint: To see the current traffic conditions, choose Show Traffic from the View option located on the menu bar.

MUSIC

Whether you're listening to millions of songs on demand or have purchased songs and albums from the iTunes Store, the Apple Music app makes it simple to organise and enjoy all of your music. When you click, you can see the next song, the songs that have come before it, and the lyrics of the current song. Use the iTunes Store to find the song you want.

You Have It In Your Library. Everything you've bought from the iTunes Store, everything you've added from the Apple Music catalogue, and anything in your personal library can be seen and played with ease. You may sort the stuff you're looking at by Songs, Artists, Albums, or Recently Added.

Peruse Apple Music's Finest Selection. To see the latest songs and exclusive releases on Apple songs, a music streaming service that costs a monthly charge, click on Browse in the sidebar. Enjoy ad-free streaming and downloading of over 50 million songs, plus a plethora of playlists to help you discover the ideal tunes for any occasion. Now you can follow musicians you like to get updates when they release new music and suggestions for artists you may like.

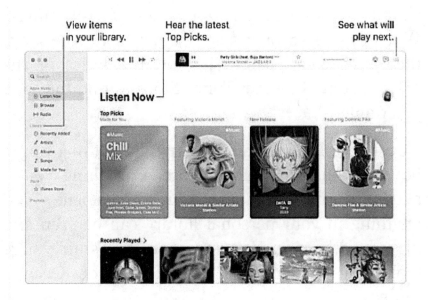

View items in your library.

Hear the latest Top Picks.

See what will play next.

Come On, Sing Along. If the song's lyrics are available, you may access them by clicking the Lyrics button on the toolbar.

Listen Up. You may listen to every episode of any programme in the Apple Music family, including Apple Music 1, live, by clicking Radio on the sidebar. Discover the wide range of stations dedicated to almost every musical style.

Just Ask Siri. Promptly state, "Please add this song to my library."

Easy Syncing. You can sync all of your music library from inside the Apple Music app. The Finder's sidebar will display any connected devices.

All you have to do is drop the media files you choose onto your mobile device. The Finder also has backup and restore capabilities for your device.

Listen Together. Join up to 32 pals in real-time music streaming with SharePlay. Gather everyone on a FaceTime call first, and then hit the SharePlay button. Simply hover your finger over the track or album you want to listen to in the Music app and press the Play button to begin playing. Anyone can add or move tracks in the shared music queue, and everyone can hear the same music at the same time. They can also share the controls for playing the music. You can still hear each other well, even in very noisy environments, thanks to adaptive volume.

Note: SharePlay requires macOS 12.3 or later on Macs and iPadOS 15.4 or later on iPads. A membership may be required to access some SharePlay-compatible applications. Some nations or areas may not have access to all features or material.

To Purchase, Visit The ITunes Store. Go to the iTunes Store on the sidebar if you want to purchase your songs. (Select Music > Settings, then select General. Then, pick Show iTunes Store if you don't see it in the sidebar.)

Tip: To listen to and manage your music while doing other things on your Mac, use MiniPlayer. It opens a little floating window that you can drag anywhere you like. This is useful when screen real estate is at a premium. Select Window > MiniPlayer to launch MiniPlayer.

PHOTOS

Keep your picture collection current across all of your devices with photographs and iCloud Photos, where you can also organise, edit, and share your films and photographs. Displaying your finest photographs, Photos makes it simple to discover and appreciate your favourites with enhanced search capabilities. You may make expert-level edits to your photographs and videos with the help of simple editing tools. Moreover, with the new iCloud Shared Photo Library feature, you may invite up to five others to an album, and then everyone can contribute media, make comments, and see each other's edits.

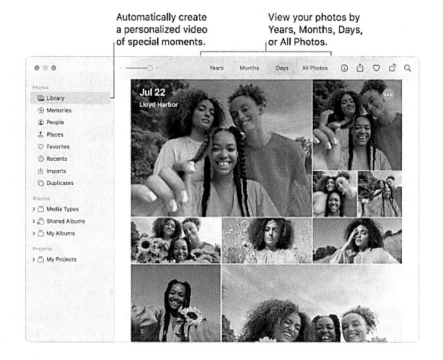

Automatically create a personalized video of special moments.

View your photos by Years, Months, Days, or All Photos.

All Of Your Images Across All Of Your Devices. If you have more than one Apple ID, you may use iCloud Photos to access, organise, and share all of your media files from any of your connected devices. All of your iOS devices will instantly display the photos you snap with your iPhone. Additionally, all of your devices will reflect whatever picture editing you do. To begin, go to System Preferences, then locate your Apple ID on the sidebar. From there, choose iCloud, and finally, toggle Photos on.

Get The iCloud Photo Library Up And Running. Make sure all family members may experience more comprehensive memories by sharing media in a separate library. The Photos app makes it easy to access both your personal and shared library items. Everyone who has access to the Shared Library may see any modifications made to the media files, such as adding or removing clips. There is a limit of five individuals per shared library that you may join.

To enable iCloud Photos and set up iCloud Shared Photo Library, you'll need to be logged in with your Apple ID. Get Started by navigating to Photos > Settings and then clicking the Shared Library link. Participants may be added immediately or at a later time if desired. The Shared Library allows you to choose which of your previous photographs and videos to upload. You may choose to include all of them, those with a certain person or shot after a specific date, or even manually pick which ones to add. Once you've configured the Shared Library, you'll be able to see photos from either your Personal Library, the Shared Library, or both libraries simultaneously in Photos.

Enhance Your Shared Library With Media Files. By selecting "Move to Shared Library" with the Control key when you right-click an image or video in your Personal Library, you may transfer it to your Shared Library. Go to images > Settings, then click on the Shared Library tab. Check the box for Shared Library recommendations. Then, pick "Add People" to get recommendations of images or videos with chosen individuals. This will enable you to utilise the ideas for potential additions to your library.

Distributed To You. Photos sent to you by contacts in your Contacts list will show up in the Shared with You area of your Photos app as soon as they arrive in your Messages. Your collection displays photos from events you attended or other moments you are likely to cherish. You may launch Messages and continue the discussion by clicking the message bubble on a picture while viewing them in the Photos app.

Revise Expertly. Make your films and photographs stand out with these simple but powerful editing tools. To make quick edits to your movie or picture, use the editing tools up top. Press Edit to get more advanced editing options, and then utilise Smart Sliders for polished results. Photos and videos may have filters applied, flipped, boosted in exposure, and cropped.

Read And Respond To Text. You may use Live Text to read text in online and computer pictures. On a Mac, you can cut and paste text from photos into other files, or you may click on images to access their corresponding websites or phone numbers. Use Control-clicking on selected text and then clicking Translate to bring up the translation. Some languages are not supported. Read the macOS User Guide on how to use Translate on a Mac.

Relive Wonderful Times. Celebrations like birthdays, anniversaries, and vacations are better remembered with photos. Live Photos and videos start playing as you go through your picture collection, bringing everything to life. By selecting Memories from the sidebar, you may have Photos make a personalised movie with transitions, titles, music, and moods that you can then share with others. Every single one of your iCloud Photo-enabled devices has access to your Memories.

Locate The Desired Item. Displaying just the highest quality images from your collection, Photos also conceals copies, receipts, and screenshots. You may sort your images by year, month, or day using the options up top, or you can just click All images to see them all at once. photographs recognises scenes, objects, and people in your movies and photographs, allowing you to search your library by subject, date, persons you've identified, captions you've added, and location (if given). Searching for photographs is also possible using Siri and Spotlight.

Just Ask Siri. "Show me photos of Ursula," you could say.

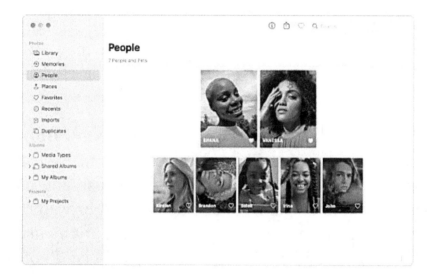

Subjects, Locations, And Objects. Many things in your images may be recognised by Visual Lookup. Select items and scenes in a picture by swiping up or by clicking the information icon. Get a better understanding of well-known works of art and sites from throughout the globe, as well as flora and fauna, literary works, and animal breeds. Click the

Favourites button on a person's picture to have their photo always shown at the top of the People album. In the Places album, you may see a map that shows all of your images annotated with their locations. Additional photographs from a certain area may be seen by zooming in on the map.

Tip: Any picture may have its location information added to it. Press the Information button while looking at the picture, then choose Assign a Location, and then begin typing. You may either enter in the address and hit Return, or choose it from the list.

Explore Your Creativity With Live Photos. You may use Live Photos' Loop effect to have the action loop endlessly, or Bounce to pause and play the animation again. An average stream or waterfall may be transformed into a piece of beauty by using Long Exposure to blur motion in your Live Photos, giving them a professional DSLR appearance.

REMINDERS

Using Reminders, keeping track of all your to-dos is simpler than ever before. Make a list of everything you need to buy, complete job tasks, or anything else you can think of to keep track of. To make your reminders fit with your workflow, utilise the versatile tools like Tags and Custom Smart Lists.

You can even store lists as templates to use them again and again. Another useful feature for teamwork is the ability to share lists.

You May Add Or Change A Reminder. Simply click the Add button on the top right or use the space below an existing list of reminders to add a new one. Put a date or place, some remarks, and tags on your reminder. To provide further information, such an early reminder to get a second notice for a significant event, click the Information button.

Make Your Own Unique Smart Lists. Your future reminders will be automatically sorted in Smart Lists according to priority, date, time, tags, location, and flags. Select "Make into Smart List" from the Add List menu, then add filters to create a custom smart list.

Make A List Of Necessities. When you make a grocery list, the products will be automatically sorted into categories like Meat, Produce, and Snacks & Candy. After clicking Add List, a drop-down option will appear; from there, choose Groceries to begin making your shopping list.

Note: Availability of grocery lists may vary by language.

Make A Copy Of A List To Use Later. If you make a list once and then wish to use it again, you can save the original as a template. Click File > Save as Template after selecting the list from the sidebar.

View Upcoming Events. Items are grouped according to time and date in the Today and Scheduled lists found on the sidebar. Make sure you're never behind the times by staying on top of forthcoming reminders.

Keep Your Reminders In Order. To create a subtask, just drag one reminder over another, or right-click on the reminder and choose Command-]. To maintain a clear picture, you have the option to either expand or compress your subtasks.

Make a new area in your reminder list to store reminders that are similar to each other. Edit > Add Section is the way to proceed, or select Manage Sections > Add Section if you currently have one section created. Select the section's bottom to find the placeholder reminder, and then begin typing to add a reminder to that part.

Select File > New Group to create a new sidebar grouping for all of your reminder lists. You are free to choose the name of the group. Simply drag more listings into the group or delete existing ones to make room.

See Reminders Organised In Columns Or Lists. For a fresh perspective on your to-do list, try seeing your reminders as columns. Select "as Columns" from the View menu. Complete reminders, move them to other areas, and add information with ease since each section becomes a column. Click the Add button to add a new column while you're using columns. Using columns with Smart Lists is not possible.

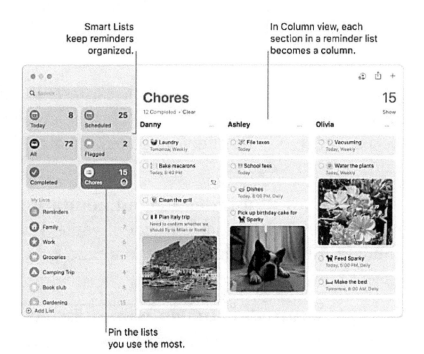

Smart Lists keep reminders organized.

In Column view, each section in a reminder list becomes a column.

Pin the lists you use the most.

Make A List Together. In Messages or Mail, you may invite someone to work on a list with you, or you can just share the link. To send a message, send an email, or create an invitation link, just click the share button. Sharing in Messages instantly adds all participants to the recipients list. Once you've sent an invitation, you can manage cooperation and keep tabs on activities by clicking the Collaborate option.

Make A Tasked List. Share your lists with others and make sure they get a notice by assigning them a reminder. Divide up the work and make sure that everyone is aware of their role. Select the sharing method you like after clicking the Share button on the navigation bar to distribute a list.

Check Out Your Progress. You can see all of your completed reminders, along with the date you checked them off, in the Completed Smart List located on your sidebar.

Receive Email Reminder Recommendations. Siri can identify potential reminders while you're communicating with someone in Mail and provide ideas for how to generate them.

Insert A Reminder In No Time. To add a reminder fast, use natural language. If you want to remember yourself to take Amy to football every

Wednesday at 5 PM, for instance, you may write it down.

Just Ask Siri. Promptly state, "When I leave here, please remind me to stop at the grocery store."

SAFARI

With revolutionary privacy features like passkeys, Safari is a robust and efficient browser. Safari remains same across all of your iOS devices—iPhone, Mac, and iPad—as long as you use the same Apple ID to access iCloud. This includes your tab bar, extensions, and home screen.

Find More Information By Beginning Your Search. As soon as you begin entering a term or URL, Safari will display websites that match your search criteria, along with some suggestions. You may also use the shortcuts on your Safari home page to access your most used or favorited websites. Press Command-T or click the Add button on the far right of Safari's window to create a new tab and begin a new search.

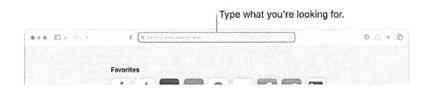

Hint: To access accessible sites in Reader mode, which eliminates advertisements and other distractions, click the Reader symbol located to the left of the search box. Click the Font icon in Reader mode to change the font and colour.

Quickly See The Contents Of The Tab. Tabs with favicons, which are logos or symbols connected with websites, make it easy to recognise a page quickly. If you hover your mouse over a tab, a preview of the page's contents will appear.

Look At The Sidebar. You may access your Reading List, Bookmarks, Tab Groups, and Shared with You from the sidebar. To access the links, click on the symbol on the sidebar. If you click the Tab pop-up menu next to Tab Groups in the sidebar, you can expand Tab Groups to view all of your tabs within a group.

The current profile; click to open a window in a different profile.

Maintain A Distinct Profile For Each Site You Visit. Make a "School" profile and a "Personal" profile in Safari to segregate your various data, such as your bookmarks, history, and Tab Groups. After selecting Safari > Create Profile, click New Profile. In the next window, you can give your profile a name, choose a colour scheme, and add a symbol. To add a new profile to an existing one, just click the Add button.

Hint: when the Translate button displays in the address box of a webpage in Safari, click it to quickly translate that webpage. Not all languages or areas have access to the translation capabilities. Safari:

Web Page Translation has a rundown of all the languages that are now supported.

Use Tab Groups For Organisation. If you want to keep track of the websites you visit while researching for a project or trip, you may establish a Tab Group. If you want to build a group from the tabs that are already open in the sidebar, you can do that by clicking the Add Tab Group button and then choosing New Tab Group. To create a new Tab Group with many open tabs, use Command + click on each tab you want to include, and then click the Add Tab Group button.

Within Messages, you have the ability to extend an invitation to work together on a Tab Group. All participants in the thread will be instantly joined to the Tab Group. In the sidebar, locate the Tab Group you want to share. Click the More Options icon next to it. From the menu, choose Share Tab Group. Finally, click Messages. When you create a Tab Group and share it with others, they may add tabs to it and you can see the page they are on right now.

Note: You may view your tabs from any device as long as it is connected into iCloud with the same Apple ID. This includes tab groups.

Find Further Features. Safari extensions allow you to customise your surfing experience by adding functionality to the browser. Find discount codes, improve your language, and swiftly save material from your favourite websites using extensions that prevent advertisements. To access the App Store's extensions area, go to Safari > Safari Extensions. There, you'll see featured Safari extensions and categories like "Browse Better," "Read with Ease," "Top Free Apps," and more. Go into Safari's preferences and toggle the extensions on. To enable extensions, go to the Extensions tab and tick the boxes.

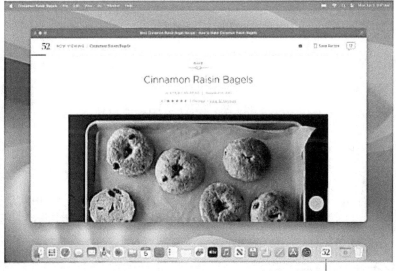

Web app appears
in the Dock.

Transform The Websites You Love Into Web Applications. To make it easier to retrieve and keep track of any website alerts, you may save a website to the Dock. After opening the webpage in Safari, go to the bottom right of the window and find the Share icon. Click on it. Then, pick Add to Dock to build a web app. Click Add once you've entered a name.

Use Apple Pay To Pay For Your Transaction. using Apple Pay on your MacBook Air, you may buy online using Safari in a way that is simple, safe, and confidential. Simply tap gently on the MacBook Air's Touch ID sensor to use Apple Pay on online purchases. You may also use your Apple Watch or iPhone to verify the payment.

No matter how many times you use Apple Pay, the company will never keep a record of your card details or disclose them with the retailer.

Note: Not every country or area supports Apple Pay or Apple Card. To learn more about Apple Pay, visit the Apple Pay website. Apple Pay partner banks is an article in Apple Support that lists the current card issuers. Check out Apple Card Support for further details.

Using Passkeys, You May Secure Your Data.
If you prefer not to use a password while signing in to websites using Touch ID or Face ID, a passkey may help. Passkeys are compatible with devices that aren't Apple products. Using passkeys—which are maintained in your iCloud keychain—is much more secure than two-factor authentication since it protects you against phishing and data breaches. A set of contacts may also have access to your passkeys.

You need to enable Password & Keychain in Cloud Settings in order to utilise passkeys. Select "Save Passkey" when prompted to do so when you log into a website. Use your iPhone, iPad, or Touch ID to log in. Follow the steps outlined in "Sign in to an account on your Mac with a passkey" to create and use a passkey.

Surf The Web Without Risk. Safari alerts you if it detects a website that isn't safe or that could be attempting to steal your personal information. In addition to protecting you from online monitoring, Safari also makes your Mac less identifiable via fingerprinting. To combat cross-site tracking, Intelligent Tracking Prevention employs state-of-the-art machine learning and on-device intelligence to detect and delete trackers' residual data.

Enjoy Your Privacy. Select File > New Private Window to open a new window that is only visible to you. A login or Touch ID is required to unlock your private window when you close it. By default, Safari remembers your browser history when you switch to private browsing. However, if you enable this feature, Safari will do more to stop websites from monitoring you, including removing tracking codes from URLs and blocking known trackers from loading entirely.

To see which websites are using cross-site trackers that Safari is blocking, click the Privacy Report button on the left side of the active tab. This will give you a better idea of how each site handles your privacy. To get a privacy report that goes into more depth on the website's active trackers, click the Full Report button.

Hide Your Email Address. If you have an iCloud+ membership, you may generate an unlimited supply of random email addresses for use in any situation where you might require one, such as filling out a website form. Any messages received to the address you set up for a website using Hide My Email will be redirected to your own inbox. A Hide My Email address allows you to receive emails without revealing your real email address, and you have the option to deactivate it whenever you choose.

SHORTCUTS

With the Shortcuts app, you may activate Siri or click a button to swiftly complete multi-step activities. You may make shortcuts to go to the next event in your calendar, copy and paste content across apps, and much more. If you need to execute several stages in a process quickly, you may use the Shortcuts Gallery to find pre-made shortcuts or create your own by combining applications.

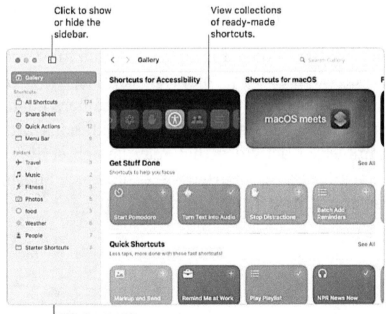

Click to show or hide the sidebar.

View collections of ready-made shortcuts.

View and organize your shortcuts in the sidebar.

A Collection Of Potential Outcomes. The Gallery is a great place to look for shortcuts or just browse. There are sets of commonly used tasks for which you may get starter shortcuts. The gallery's sidebar displays My Shortcuts, where you can see all of your created shortcuts as well as any pre-made shortcuts you choose or modify. Press the Sidebar button to reveal or conceal the Gallery sidebar.

Design Your Own Shortcut Keys. Make your desired action a shortcut by dragging it from the right-hand list into the left-hand shortcut editor once you've created a new shortcut. Similar to the phases in a task, actions are the fundamental units of a shortcut. Pick from a variety of options, such opening the Photos app to retrieve the most recent photo, making a new folder, or copying the current URL from Safari. Rounding a number, enabling aeroplane mode, and doing computations are all examples of activities that may launch scripts. To ensure that your shortcut is completed, Shortcuts also offers "next action" options.

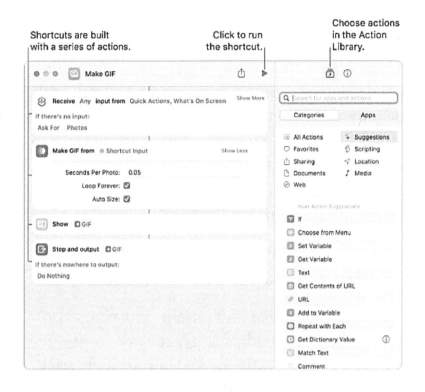

Shortcuts are built with a series of actions.

Click to run the shortcut.

Choose actions in the Action Library.

Streamlining Your Existing Shortcuts. The fastest method to do something is to use Siri to execute a shortcut. Both the Finder and the Services menu may have shortcuts added to them. After you double-click a shortcut, go to the Shortcut Details menu and choose Use as Quick Action.

Just Ask Siri. An example sentence may be: "Text last image."

Create, Sync, And Share Shortcuts. When you use the same Apple ID across all of your devices, your shortcuts will be automatically synced. All of your devices will instantly update to reflect any changes you make on one. You may also get shortcuts that other people have shared with you and share shortcuts that others have shared with you. Simply double-click the shortcut, go to the Share menu, and choose the desired sharing method. On the sidebar of the Share Sheet, you can also create shortcuts to frequently used tasks.

TIPS AND TRICKS
1. Open A Copy A File By Default

If you often utilise document templates on your Mac, Stationery Pad is a great way to eliminate a step in your workflow. An old Finder trick that keeps the original file unaltered is to have the parent programme open a duplicate of the file by default. Create skeleton HTML/CSS files, simplify basic Photoshop tasks, or get a hand with Word document invoicing with the aid of Stationery Pad's template feature. It supports almost every file format.

To use it, choose the desired file to use as a template by right-clicking (Ctrl-click), then choose Get Info. In the General section, locate the Stationery Pad checkbox and check it. Finally, to dismiss the Get Info box, touch the red traffic light button. When you double-click the template file again, Finder will make a duplicate and open it without touching the original.

Stationery Pad isn't very well-known anymore, but it's a great substitute for manually modifying templates and risking file overwriting with the "Save As..." command.

2. Get Additional Options For Preview File Formats

By selecting more than one format from the Format dropdown menu when you want to save or export in Preview, you may open a wider variety of files.

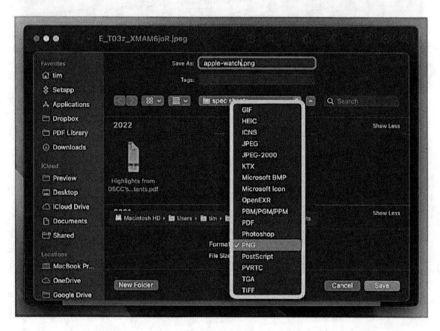

3. Return To The Search Results Page In Safari

For example, with Safari, you may use the address bar to enter a search term in order to hunt for information on a certain issue. In the search results, you click on the first link since it seems promising. On the landing page, you come across another link pertaining to a similar subject, so you proceed to click on both of them. Then you see another link that interests you and click on it to see what it has to offer. Before you know it, you've become sidetracked by a completely other topic, and you've wasted a lot of time clicking links and navigating the web without gaining any insight into your initial search.

If you're acquainted with that, Safari SnapBack is here to assist you. This will spare you the trouble of going back to the first set of search results or sifting through your browser history to find the page from which you started your most recent web adventure. Under History -> Search Results in Safari's menu bar, you'll find it. SnapBack, or even better, using the shortcut key combination Command + Option + S.

Please be aware that SnapBack can only be utilised if your misguided surfing happened in the same tab as the search, thus if a link you clicked on created a new tab and you proceeded to browse in it, you will not be able to use the SnapBack menu option. Additionally, you may only do the search from the address bar of Safari or the designated search engine's website.

4. Tame Hot Corners With Modifier Key

You may assign specific actions to each of the four corners of your macOS screen using the Hot Corners feature. This way, you can access system-wide features like Mission Control, Notification Centre, the Screen Saver, and more with a single click. A quick and easy way to access these often used functionalities is with a single click of the mouse. Not so fun is inadvertently setting off a Hot Corner, which may cause all sorts of naughty desktop behaviour including programme windows scattering randomly. Fortunately, you can control Hot Corner's actions using modifier keys.

To access Hot Corners, go to System Preferences >
Desktop & Dock, then scroll down to the bottom of
the page. Select the screen corner you want to utilise
as a Hot Corner from the drop-down option in the
resulting dialogue box. After then, press and hold a
modifier key until a drop-down menu appears; then,
choose a function to put in the Hot Corner. As an
example, we're going to use the Shift-Command.
You must now remember to hold down the modifier
key(s) while dragging the mouse pointer towards a
Hot Corner the next time you want to use it;

otherwise, the action you set to that corner will not activate.

5. Display Dock Apps With The Most Recent Updates

You may add a divider to the right-hand side of your Mac's Dock and show any recently used programmes that aren't permanently docked by using an option named "Show recent applications in Dock" in macOS. You can find this setting under System Settings -> Desktop & Dock. This setting will only display the last three applications that were open, even if you have subsequently dismissed them. On the other hand, if your workflow requires you to utilise many applications in succession, there is a method to make it display more.

To change the amount of recently launched applications shown in your Dock, you may simply copy and paste instructions into Terminal. Press Enter after pasting the following into the command prompt in a Terminal window (the programme is located in /Applications/Utilities/):

In this example, you can set the number of recently launched applications to show in the Dock after the divider to 10 using the -int parameter. The number may be adjusted to your liking, and the option to display three applications again can be found in the second command with the -int 3 option.

6. Center-Mount Window Resizing

Instead of dragging the window's edges or corners to resize it, you may start in the window's centre and adjust its proportions by holding down the Option key.

7. Get Notified Of New Emails From Vips In A Special Way

To enable new message alerts from VIPs in Apple Mail, go to Mail -> Settings... on the main menu, then choose the General tab. From the New message notifications selection list, choose VIPs. Even while this is a great method to set up VIP alerts, it will also stop you from getting notifications for any other communications that arrive in your mailbox. Instead, you should create a rule in Mail that triggers an action, such playing a sound or bouncing the Dock icon, whenever you get a message from someone on your VIP list.

Select the Rules tab in Mail's Settings, and then choose Add Rule. Choose an option from the dropdown menu for "If" and then give your rule a name in the Description box. Indicate that the sender is a VIP in the first condition. (Another choice here is Account if you want notifications for a particular individual.)

Pick Play Sound from the first dropdown under "Perform the following actions:" after that. (You also have the option of using the Bounce Icon in Dock.) When prompted, choose an audio file to play from the second drop-down menu under "Perform the following actions:". Last but not least, hit OK and then Apply. Now that the rule is in place, you will get a distinct alert for each VIP message, allowing you to easily identify it from other new message alerts.

8. View Notes On App Windows Floating

One feature of macOS's Notes app is the ability to "float" notes over other windows, keeping them visible even when other apps are closed. In the middle of writing a report or essay, for instance, this is a handy method to cite a previous remark. Additionally, it is helpful if you want to jot down notes when doing research on the internet.

To make a note floating in the Notes app, open it in a new window by double-clicking it. Then, from the menu bar, choose Window -> Keep on Top. Now, even when you use Stage Manager to move between applications, the note will stay at the top of the list. Keep in mind that while another programme is in fullscreen mode, your floating notes will not be able to share the screen with it.

9. Organise Your Files, Applications, And Folders On The Finder Tip Bar

Here's how to customise the Finder window toolbar with quick links to your favourite apps, files, and folders: Hold down the Command (⌘) key and drop the item into an empty spot in the toolbar once you start dragging it inside the Finder window.

10. Get To The System Preferences You Need Fast

To access some capabilities on your Mac, you may hit the function keys that have icons written on them. To change the level, for instance, hit the F11 or F12 keys, which are labelled with speaker images.

By simultaneously pressing Option and one of these keys, you may quickly access the feature-specific options in System Settings. To access the Sound window, for example, press Option-F11/12.

11.   Sick Of Keyboarding?

If you're using macOS Sonoma and want to utilise Dictation at the same time, you won't have any problems keeping your train of thought uninterrupted.

What this means is that you may continue typing even after pressing the Dictation shortcut, which can be customised under System Settings -> Keyboard. You may finish what you were typing by speaking it aloud anytime your fingers become tired.

12.   Have   Safari   Tabs   Close   Automatically

Mac OS X has the ability to automatically shut Safari tabs depending on the time you last visited them. From the main menu, choose Safari -> Settings..., and then locate the Tabs area.

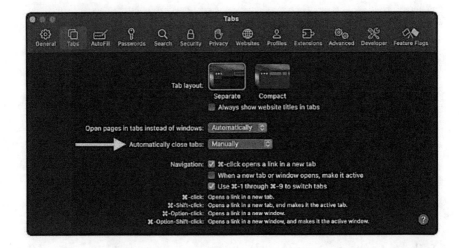

Just underneath "Automatically close tabs" you'll see three choices to set the browser to automatically shut tabs after a certain amount of time has passed that have not been viewed: one day, one week, and one month.

13.   Use Finder To Locate Downloads Of Mail Attachments

In macOS Sonoma, a new mail symbol appears next to the file name when you open it in Finder after downloading it from Mail. This indicates that the file is an attachment to an email.

The contextual menu that appears when you right-click an attachment even has a "Reply to [name of sender]" option; selecting this will bring up the Mail compose window, where you can input your reply.

14.   Transfer Images Quickly Using An Icloud Link

With the latest update to macOS, Sonoma, you can now generate an iCloud link to share media files saved in iCloud Photos.

To copy an iCloud link, just choose one image or many images, click the Share button, and then choose Copy iCloud Link. Then you can paste it into an email or message.